happily ever
laughter

To Julie

happily ever ♥
laughter

*discovering the lighter
side of marriage*

*Kendra Smiley
(John 8:32)*

KEN DAVIS
GENERAL EDITOR

Tyndale House Publishers, Inc.
Carol Stream, Illinois

Livingstone project staff include: Neil Wilson, Dave Veerman, and Dana Niesluchowski
Editor: Marianne Hering
Cover design by Stephen Vosloo
Cover photograph copyright © by Ricky Molloy/photolibrary. All rights reserved.
Back cover photograph of umbrella copyright © by Anton Zhukov/iStockphoto.
All rights reserved.

Library of Congress Cataloging-in-Publication Data
Happily ever laughter : discovering the lighter side of marriage / Ken Davis, general editor.
    p. cm.
 "Focus on the Family."
 ISBN 978-1-58997-580-4
 1. Marriage—Religious aspects—Christianity—Humor. I. Davis, Ken, 1946-
 BV4596.M3H37 2010
 242'.644—dc22

                              2010000769

ISBN: 978-1-58997-580-4

Printed in the United States of America
 4 5 6 7 8 9/ 15 14

Dedicated to my children and grandchildren,
who have brought so much happiness and laughter to my life.
—Ken Davis

Contents

Welcome to Happily Ever Laughter

Ken Davis

A husband who didn't know how to do housework decided to wash his sweatshirt. Seconds after he stepped into the laundry room, he shouted to his wife, "Hey, what setting do I use on the washing machine?"

She answered, "Well, it depends. What does it say on your shirt?"

He yelled back, "Denver Broncos!"

You know, my wife and I consistently experience this kind of miscommunication. For example, recently Diane has been asking me to share my feelings. While waiting at a stoplight the other day, I spotted one of my favorite donut shops across the street. Because I'm trying to lose weight, I shouldn't go there anymore. Suddenly it hit me—that's a feeling, and I decided to share it. So wistfully I sighed, "Dunkin' Donuts."

Diane said, a little indignantly, "What?"

I repeated, a bit louder and a bit irritated myself, "Dunkin' Donuts."

This time she said it louder, "What?"

I have to admit, at that point I lost it. "What part of 'Dunkin'

Donuts' don't you understand!" I shouted. To which she responded, with the same volume, "Don't condone what?"

I guess she expected me to actually pull up to the shop and mime eating a donut before she would understand what I was talking about.

Today she came in the door from a trip to the grocery store and a few other places. We had talked about her picking up a DVD to watch, so I asked, "Did you get *Bourne Ultimatum*?"

"What?" she said. Evidently she saw me roll my eyes, because she responded defensively, "I don't know what 'porno tomato' is." Then we both started laughing. I caught my breath just in time to tell her, "I'm not going to try to explain it to you."

You know, Diane says that I expect her to read my mind. Well, hello! Wasn't that part of the marriage ceremony? Nope. But laughter certainly was part of the deal. It's often the glue that helps us keep things in perspective—laughter and a healthy awareness that neither of us is entirely OK.

The contributions that fill this book are intended to shine the spotlight of laughter on marriage, in hopes of helping us remember the fine line between deep satisfaction coupled with joy on the one hand and dissatisfaction coupled with joylessness on the other. Marriages need the kind of laughter that comes out of joy. And joy always involves choices we make. We have good reasons, even in marriage, to choose joy! What you will read in these pages are some examples of married people who are choosing joy—and laughing as they do. They are deciding to see what is funny in life even during uncomfortable and difficult times.

Deciding to choose joy doesn't mean we pretend that life isn't hard. Joy never says, "I just love beating myself on the thumb with a hammer because it feels so good when I stop!" Joy says, "Yeah, that hurt. It hurt something fierce! It broke a good streak of perfect behavior I had going that day." As the thumb throbbed and began to take on gigantic proportions, a bad word formed back in the dark regions of my brain. You know the feeling. You might already be laughing, bracing yourself for a bad word, or trying to guess which bad word was lurking in my mind. The word you're thinking of will do fine.

The point I'm trying to make is not that we should come up with more colorful bad words but that we have a lot of traits in common. We *do* demonstrate bad aim with hammers. And we curiously connect our throbbing thumb with a bad word, as if one is going to fix the other. These odd tendencies provoke laughter, and we all have a deep need for laughter—for joy. We need to see that just because life is difficult doesn't mean there are no more reasons to laugh. You won't find any bad words in this book, but you will find some valuable lessons in joy.

Marriage is an important and serious commitment, and laughter is a crucial part of keeping marriage alive. *Happily Ever Laughter* is the right kind of title for this book. It says a lot more than you think when you first read it. When I first heard it, the phrase hit me like those punch lines that work because they slightly alter reality, like asking someone, "Would you rather die or just lose your life?" I was thinking *after,* but my ears were registering *laughter*. It took me a second to make the connection. It made me smile. This book challenges the widely accepted idea that marriage should be about living *happily ever after* and replaces it with the much better and more achievable idea of living *happily ever laughter*.

So enjoy these stories. If you and your spouse read them together, you will find different parts funny. When I'm telling stories about our marriage, Diane laughs at the oddest parts . . .

Make sure you welcome laughter in your marriage. It will go a long way toward helping you live happily.

What I Want in a Man As the Years Go By

Ken Davis

Sometimes it's good to have realistic expectations. For example, here's something my wife, Diane, wrote...

Here's the list of things I wanted in a man before I got married:
- Handsome, charming, stylish dresser, thoughtful, in great physical condition, and romantic

Here's how I revised the list at age thirty:
- Nice looking; opens car doors; is a good listener; works out some and is in decent shape; remembers anniversaries, birthdays, and other important events in our lives; and is romantic at least once a week

Here's what I wanted in a man at forty-one:
- Not too ugly, waits until I'm in the car before driving away, acts as if he's listening, holds stomach in, remembers to put the toilet seat down, and often shaves on the weekends

And the revised list at fifty-two:

- Usually combs hair that's left, asks if I'd like a ride, stays awake when I'm talking, wears a shirt that covers his stomach, rarely forgets my name, and sometimes shaves on the weekends

The new list for sixty-three:

- Keeps nose- and ear-hair trimmed, can still drive, doesn't make bodily noises or scratch in public, usually wears fresh underwear and matching socks, remembers why he went into a room, and usually shaves

Here's what I will want at seventy-four:

- Looks don't scare small children, can still find the bathroom, usually wears some clothes, likes soft foods, knows where he left his teeth, and can remember that it *is* the weekend

Finally, what I will want at age eighty-five:

- Is breathing and can hit the toilet

The older you are, the easier to meet the expectations!

LAUGH LESSON

Aging may not seem like a laughing matter, but you'll be much better off if you *do* learn to laugh with the changes that age brings. Then you're not so apt to be disappointed with each other. And besides, nose hair really *is* kind of funny . . .

Bearer of the Ring

Bob Stromberg

The marriage begins with the wedding, and young Bob Stromberg gives us the inside view from one participant.

The Event: My sister Sally and I at our Aunt Audrey's wedding
The Date: August 22, 1959
The Photographer: My father

I am seven years old and I am sharp! *Sharp* is a word I've just learned in this context and never before used to describe myself. A couple of hours ago, before the wedding, my mother pinned a flower on my jacket. Then licking her fingers and flattening down my eyebrows, she said, "Young man, you are dapper dandy." I understand why she said it. After all, she's never seen me in a tuxedo before—what my new uncle Ted calls a "penguin suit." She was surprised and quite impressed with my appearance, so she called me "dapper dandy." It means that I am very handsome, and indeed I am—particularly today as I am wearing white dress shoes . . . unscuffed!

Though I appreciate my mother's comment, my enthusiasm is tempered by the fact that she also made a terrible fuss over how beautiful my sister Sally looks in her flower-girl dress. Please don't misunderstand me. I, too, am impressed with the dress. It's pretty big—much like Cinderella's gown at the ball—and the outfit includes a stylish little crown with a table doily. It is an impressive ensemble, though I must say I think Sally herself looks much like she always does. But, hey . . . if Mom thinks that she is beautiful . . . well . . . fine.

I am not beautiful, though, and I'm not dapper dandy either. I am sharp. I know this because before the wedding my new uncle Ted (whose outfit is just like mine only much bigger) looked at me and said, "Whoa, Bobby." He grabbed me by the shoulders and squared me off for a good look. "I gotta say it. You, my man, are sharp."

What was I supposed to say? "Oh no, I'm not sharp. I'm dapper dandy." No . . . I'm happy to be sharp and proud to be a ring bearer.

I remember well when Aunt Audrey and her boyfriend, Ted, asked Sally and me to be in their wedding party. By the way, don't be fooled by the term *wedding party*. It might sound fun, but that's just so the two people getting married can get friends to come. It's no party at all. For one thing, it doesn't just take one night. It takes practically a whole weekend. When you join a wedding party, you are committing yourself to an evening without friends, sitting in a church, and rehearsing for the actual party that happens the next day. And even that is more like going to church than a party. The whole deal is pretty serious—not a lot of fun.

Audrey is our favorite aunt. She is quite beautiful. She has eyeglasses with real gems glued in the corners. She used to be a majorette in high school and wore white cowboy boots with a short skirt while twirling a baton. I don't think I could ever do that. But I could show you the boots and baton, because I know right where they are in her old bedroom closet at my grandparents' house. I really liked her boyfriend, Ted, a lot too. He has curly hair and is what is called "a giant." I knew he'd make a great uncle.

Audrey asked if Sally would be her flower girl and then went on to explain what the job entails. Sally went crazy with excitement, probably because all she had to do is walk in with a bunch of flowers, stand there for three or four hours, and then walk back out again. As long as she didn't have to pee or pass out, she could hardly fail.

> For two people in a marriage to live together
> day after day is unquestionably the one miracle
> that the Vatican has overlooked.
>
> —Bill Cosby

Then Ted asked me if I would be his ring bearer. My job description was a bit more ominous. I would be entrusted with the actual wedding ring in the "best of view" at the back of the church. I would need to carry the ring clear to the pulpit in the front of the church—a distance of nearly four hundred yards. To make matters worse, I would not be permitted to touch the ring with my hands but would balance it upon a tiny satin pillow. I am only seven. My knowledge of fabrics is limited, but even I know that satin is slippery.

I was sitting on the couch in our living room. Ted was in a chair on the other side of the coffee table, waiting for my answer. "I'm wondering about the material on that pillow," I said. "Why does it have to be satin?"

"I'm not really sure," he said. "It's just always satin."

"Yeah, I understand that," I said, "but I was wondering if we could maybe use a scratchy wool or burlap. Even corduroy would work fine."

"Nope," he said laughing, "I'm pretty sure Audrey wants the pillow to be satin."

"Rubber might be nice," I countered.

"No," he said, "I think we'll stick with satin. The pillow's already been ordered."

"How big is the ring?" I asked.

From the other side of the room, Audrey held up her hand, flashing a band with a diamond setting. "Just a little bigger than this one," she said.

I didn't want to say it, but I was concerned about the heat registers in the floor just inside the "best of view." If I tripped, that ring could slide off that slippery satin and fall down into a register. If that happened, it would be lost forever, like one of my mother's earrings and several of my peppermint candies.

"How much did the ring cost?" I asked nervously.

The adults laughed, and my mother said, "Bobby, it's not polite to ask how much things cost."

"How much do you think it cost?" Ted said.

"Well, I don't know. Maybe a million dollars?" I said. More laughter from the adults.

My father spoke up. "I'll tell you something. That ring is worth far more than a million. That ring is gonna cost Ted every bit of freedom he ever had."

More laughter.

I never did find out for sure how much it cost, but I'm guessing it was about a million and one hundred dollars.

Ted was waiting for an answer.

"Yes," I said finally. "I will do it. I will bear your ring." I felt the weight of great responsibility settle on my young, narrow shoulders.

Now I'm standing next to Sally on the steps of the church after the wedding. She is still holding her flowers. She did fine considering the little that was required. I, on the other hand, performed excellently.

Before we walk out the door, a lady says to me, "You did a great job, young man." Then reaching for a basket on the back pew, she says, "Oh, wait . . . I have something just for you." I am excited, as I'd not been expecting payment for my services. The lady turns toward me and empties a napkin full of rice into my hands. I have no idea why.

"Gee, thanks," I say. "You shouldn't have."

Sally looks a bit miffed.

We walk out the door. Our dad, the wedding photographer, is standing on the sidewalk with his camera. "Wait you two. Hold it right there!" he shouts. So we do, and a bunch of other people start snapping pictures too. I'm feeling a bit awkward, trying hard not to spill any rice. It's okay, though. I can handle it because I am sharp.

♥

More than fourteen years later I stood at the front of another church and, once again, I was sharp—this time in a polyester brown tuxedo with a yellow ruffled shirt. One could hardly look sharper in 1974. I stood beside the love of my life—a beautiful girl, only eighteen years old. She wore a wedding dress. Her little brother walked down the aisle with a tiny satin pillow holding our gold rings. He was far less disciplined than I'd been years before. Had the rings not been attached, he surely would have lost them. A pastor asked me a series of questions, each one requiring a response. At the end I answered, "Yes. I will." What I meant was *Yes. I will bear the ring.*

It was a far riskier pledge this time around. This ring I would bear whether sick or healthy, rich or poor—in both good times and bad. I know some who are unable to make such a commitment. They are afraid to even try. I know others who tried, some for a long while, and then gave up. I don't judge them. It is serious business bearing this ring.

I have done so for nearly four decades and will until the day I die. Years ago I worried that the ring would slip off my finger. There is no chance of that now. Whenever I remove it (which is seldom), I'm surprised to see how it has left a permanent mark in my skin—how my finger has changed its very shape to hold the ring safely. And here is the mysterious thing: Every year the ring takes on more weight, and every year it is lighter and more joyous to bear.

LAUGH LESSON

That spontaneous wedding joy needs to be preserved and nourished through the years. Your perspective on the wedding ceremony will certainly change over time. When the ring bearer becomes a ring wearer, the added significance of the role greatly increases the depth and length of responsibility—but also the joy. Savor the memories.

Adapted from Bob Stromberg's "Life on the Carousel" blog, which can be found at *www.BobStromberg.com*, along with clips from Bob's presentations, contact information, his event schedule, and more.

Here Comes the Bride

Kendra Smiley

Most newlyweds have what's called a honeymoon period—a time when they stare starry-eyed at each other and think that nothing will ever go wrong in their world. For Kendra and her husband, John, that honeymoon period lasted for just thirty seconds after they kissed at the altar . . .

"Do you, John, take Kendra to be your wife, to have and to hold from this day forward, for better, for worse, for richer, for poorer, in sickness and in health, to love and to cherish, until death do you part?"

"I do."

"Do you, Kendra, take John to be your husband, to have and to hold from this day forward, for better, for worse, for richer, for poorer, in sickness and in health, to love and to cherish, until death do you part?"

"I do."

"I now pronounce you man and wife. John, you may kiss the bride."

Close your eyes for just a minute and picture the kiss. Hear the triumphant, awe-inspiring bridal recessional as it fills the sanctuary. Imagine me, Kendra, the radiant bride in a flowing white dress standing beside my handsome husband. We turn toward the congregation of family and friends, who are smiling delightedly, a few even brushing away a tear of joy as the organ plays. (End of scene 1.)

Now fast-forward to the first conflict between us, the newlyweds.

Stop! Don't hold that fast-forward button down too long. Our first clash was not weeks later or days later or even hours later. It occurred just as we turned and took three steps back down the aisle.

> ♥   "I am" is reportedly the shortest sentence in
> ♥   the English language. Could it be that "I do" is
> ♥   the longest sentence?
> ♥
> —George Carlin

What, you may ask, could possibly cause this first quarrel a mere thirty seconds into our marriage?

To help you understand, let me describe my bridal veil. It was a full-length one that trailed elegantly behind me and was attached to a small hat perched on top of my head. The hat was secured to my hair, and I suspect to my scalp, with bobby pins—many, many bobby pins. Conservatively speaking, I would say that there were between two and three million of them doing the job. This was *not* an ideal situation.

After the pastor pronounced us husband and wife, we turned to march to the back of the church. Before we had gained much speed, John inadvertently stepped on my veil. The forward progress of the veil ceased immediately, and my entire head jerked backward.

The bobby pins held their ground (for better or for worse), but I had an instant headache. Knowing that John was unaware of the pain he had just inflicted on his new bride, I smiled bravely and said in a tense, pain-induced whisper, "Don't step on my veil again. That really hurt."

It could not have been more than another two steps before he unknowingly repeated the pain-producing act. My head jerked back once again, and in a quiet but much sterner tone, still smiling for the crowd, I simply said, "If you do that again, I'm going to have to kill you!" I am almost sure that at that moment he (1) still had no idea what he had done and (2) wondered if he had made a big mistake in those vows he'd just said! The "for worse" part was coming way too quickly!

John was oblivious, to say the least. His mind was not on my veil. In fact, in one of the informal photographs taken as we walked back down the aisle of the church, his attitude was captured exactly. He was pointing with glee at one of his college roommates. His look said it all: "I've done it! I'm married. She's crazy about me. I've survived the wedding, and now it's a quick appearance at the reception and we're off to the honeymoon. Woo-hoo!"

Obviously the last thing on his mind was the security of my veil, my hat, and my many bobby pins. What did any of those things have to do with the honeymoon? He was ready to get to the "good part."

I don't remember how we resolved that first conflict, but we must have because I obviously didn't kill him before the reception—we have now celebrated more than thirty years of marriage. That trip down the aisle was just the first of many times when we've both had to learn where to step, and to be aware when our steps might end up hurting each other.

LAUGH LESSON

Conflict is an inevitable part of marriage. It doesn't take long (in John and Kendra's case, a mere thirty seconds) before couples find themselves literally or figuratively stepping on each other's toes and causing hurt that was never intended. Marital conflict is at times over trivial matters; at other times, it is more serious. In any case, learning to communicate, to express feelings, and to really hear each other are the first steps to handling difficult situations. When conflict arises, learn to care even more about each other, and find ways to show love even while you're working through the difficulty. And if you can defuse the conflict by finding something funny about your situation, all the better.

Adapted from *Do Your Kids a Favor . . . Love Your Spouse* by Kendra Smiley with John Smiley (Moody Publishers, Chicago 2008). Used by permission. To learn more about Kendra's ministry and to contact her, visit ***www.KendraSmiley.com*** or ***www.ParentingLikeAPro.com***.

Brush with Reality

Dave Veerman

The honeymoon is only a short vacation followed by a lifetime of learning about each other. But on their honeymoon, Dave and his wife, Gail, found their differences surfacing even as they tried to play it cool . . .

We were typical newlyweds, I guess, if such a thing exists. That is, we were madly in love, overwhelmed by the wonder that we were suddenly and finally husband and wife, and fully optimistic about our future together. Yet, being very mature twenty-six-year-olds, we didn't want to get into all that mushy stuff. We weren't kids, after all, and we didn't want to be treated that way.

We decided that we would be different from other honeymooners. We wanted to appear to be a mature couple. No looking mooney-eyed at each other over our dinners, no one toasting "the newlyweds" at the resort, no giggling over my wife's new last name. In short, no one taking note that we were new to this marriage stuff. Our car bore none of the usual "Just Married" markings, and we had purged it of rice. We were determined that our actions wouldn't give us away. As far as anyone would be able to guess, we were a couple, happily married for several years and simply on vacation. We would play it totally cool.

After our first night in a nearby hotel, where we made sure to shake out all the rice embedded in our clothes, we got back on the road and headed to a resort a few hours north. At the front desk, we simply signed in as Mr. and Mrs. Veerman—so far so good, my gleaming wedding band notwithstanding.

♥ **Couples who think that marriage is a mini society**
♥ **made up of two completely equal members haven't**
♥ **thought enough about the fact that you can't**
♥ **have a democracy with two people.**

—Neil Wilson

After unpacking, we headed for dinner and the resort restaurant. No "congratulations to the newlyweds" signs, champagne toasts, or "honeymoon specials"—we seemed to be pulling it off.

After dinner, we strolled hand in hand through the downtown area, getting a feel for the place and window-shopping. Passing a drug store, Gail remarked that she needed to purchase a few toiletries, so we went inside.

I browsed a bit and then met Gail at checkout. She placed the items on the counter—shampoo, nail-polish remover, cotton balls, and a family-size tube of Crest toothpaste.

Incredulous, I blurted, none too softly, "Crest?"

Gail looked at me. "Yeah . . . ?" as she wondered what could possibly be the problem.

It seemed obvious to me. "I use Colgate!" I exclaimed more loudly than I should have, gaining the attention of nearby shoppers.

Gail's response, just as strong: "You're kidding. I've always used Crest!"

"Colgate cleans and brightens! Don't you remember the commercials? Man, I hate the taste of Crest!"

"Well, then, go buy yourself a tube of Colgate. I hate Colgate."

I turned to find the toothpaste aisle and discovered a line of people behind me, including, I'm sure, other experienced honeymooners, chuckling. Apparently they had worked out this toothpaste thing already.

Marital bliss. Could it already have been marred by something so simple? Hmmm, what other surprises lurked behind my lovely new wife's smile? What else hadn't she told me?

I needn't have worried. Oh yes, there were more surprises, but today, our separate toothpaste tubes sit side by side in the bathroom, evidence of a marriage that has long survived our differences, and reminders of a day many years ago when we blew our cover!

LAUGH LESSON

Toothpaste. Isn't it funny how the littlest things can seem so big? Sometimes couples don't know how to handle the differences that seem irreconcilable. Dave and Gail weren't going to convert to each other's brand of toothpaste, so they compromised—the beginning of what would naturally be a pattern of learning to mold their lives together. And to this day, toothpaste commercials make them laugh!

Dave is a founding partner of The Livingstone Corporation, a company that works with publishers to produce Bibles, books, and other materials. For more on Livingstone, check out *www.LivingstoneCorp.com*.

Marriage Grooming

John Branyan

Couples often reminisce about the beginning—the rehearsal, wedding, and early adjustments to each other's differences. What actually brings them together? What overcomes their natural reluctance and tendency to protect themselves from danger? The discovery that someone truly loves them sets a couple off on an adventure like no other.

After a fairly uneventful (read—not noteworthy) experience with dating relationships in high school, I wasn't anticipating a stellar romantic career in college. Then along came this amazing woman named Lori. Much to my surprise and contrary to my previous experiences with girls, she had no interest in just being my friend or thinking of me as a brother. She said, "I love you, John. I really, really love you."

She reeled me right in. I should have been suspicious, but I never saw it coming. I should have known I was in way over my head when we started to plan the wedding. I found out we would be having a wedding rehearsal. She told me, "And the day before the wedding, we'll have the rehearsal."

I asked, "Why do we need a wedding rehearsal? Is it tricky?"

"Yes," she said with great emphasis, "a wedding is tricky."

Then, I found out my part in the wedding—walk in a side door and stand, very still, in one place. We rehearsed this over and over again. By the sixth time, I had my part totally down. I had no idea of all the details that women build into the ceremony. And everything had to be done perfectly, or the whole affair would be ruined. For example, the organist had to play at the exact tempo that would allow the bridesmaids and groomsmen to link arms in the back of the church and march in perfect synchronicity down the center aisle, on that white paper we unrolled for some reason that I've never been able to figure out. I'm guessing it has something to do with the Occupational Safety and Health Administration regulations or some long-lost religious directive.

♥ **I married my wife for her looks—but not the**
♥ **ones she's giving me lately.**
♥ —unknown

And all the colors had to match. The flowers that the bridesmaids carried had to match the dresses they wore, which had to match the cummerbunds of the groomsmen's tuxes, which had to match the boutonnieres they wore, which then matched the color of the bridesmaids' contact lenses, the color of the carpeting in the car we rode in, and the color of the labels on the cans we dragged down the street. Even the color of the sky that time of year factored in somehow, along with the curvature of the earth and the way the light is refracted through a semipermeable membrane during the summer equinox. Guys from MIT in Boston flew out and did all the math.

Then the little girl came out with the flower basket, and the petals in that basket represented every color visible to the naked eye, perfectly harmonized to represent the unity that is true love. Well, that young lady had her own plan, and she started chucking those petals out left and right. She was enjoying herself until she was further instructed that the petals must be carefully tossed at a precise equidistance down the aisle. Those placements were determined by the mothers-in-law with measuring tapes to make sure that more petals didn't end up on the groom's side than on the bride's side because *that* would cause World War III.

Then there was that cute little ring bearer who came out with the wedding bands tied to a satin pillow. The rings are so very important that it just made sense to give them to a three-year-old, considering that the day before, he swallowed a nickel and two pennies.

Now, I don't mind practicing, but I just wish we had rehearsed something that was going to happen more than once. I spent hours of sweat equity on becoming the quintessential groom—a role I have mastered. I can do it in my sleep. But I've never had another chance to demonstrate my expertise. The minister has never called me to say, "Hey, John, we've just had a last-minute groom dropout. This is your big chance, buddy. Suit up and come do that voodoo that you do!"

Being the groom has turned out to be a wasted skill—like learning the metric system. You don't use that either. But remember what your teachers would say? "You've got to learn the metric system. By the time you grow up, there won't be miles, inches, or feet, or anything—the world will be metric, metric, metric!" They said metric would be everywhere. That we couldn't even buy soda pop without it—take me to your liter! Well, metric caught on like wildfire, didn't it?

I didn't mind rehearsing the wedding. I just wish we had practiced something really useful. I had so many things I needed practice on . . . so many things I didn't know how to do. Consequently, more than twenty years later, I'm still playing catch-up. I could have used practice in a thousand areas. I could have used practice in dropping off to sleep at night with a pair of subzero feet in my back. "Yikes, woman! You have just frostbitten my kidneys!" I could have used practice standing in the women's clothing department just outside the dressing room door, holding my wife's purse, trying to hang on to a shred of masculine dignity.

I realize that there are many parts of the adventure of marriage that can't really be practiced ahead of time. We learn on the job! Even getting used to each other, getting used to each other's nuances, is difficult. She's a *morning* person. The sun barely breaks over the horizon, and she's hovering over the bed. "Look, sleepyhead. The sun's up! The sky is blue, the birds are singing. It's going to be a great day—time to get up, up, up!" At six o'clock in the morning, I'd rather hear the sound of a cocked shotgun and someone yelling, "Everyone on the ground; this is a stickup!" At least robbers will let you lie down—and maybe you can sneak a pillow. The birds are singing? That is the only sound they know how to make. You know what I think? One bird gets up early and the "singing" outside the window is actually all the other birds shouting, "Will you shut up?"

Even climbing into bed together, figuring out the amount of space each person needs, takes years of practice and compromise. She's my wife. I love her. But there are still times . . . And then there are other times when I reach across and pull her close, smell her perfume, and kiss the back of her neck. Blow lightly in her ear. And then she turns her head toward me in the dark and whispers, "What are you thinkin'?"

"I don't know. What are you thinking?"

She pauses and says, "I was just thinking that if we fold the dish towels smaller, they will fit more efficiently into the kitchen drawer!"

To which my response is "That's exactly what I was thinking!" Then
I add, "Let's go do it now! Maybe while we're up I can do some spackling, too!"

LAUGH LESSON

The fact that two people have found and chosen each other for a lifetime of lessons ought to be a never-ending source of amazement, and a
continual source of delight. From the discovery of mutual interest, the
decision to marry, the details of the wedding, to all the rest of it, marriage will provide daily opportunities for cooperation and learning. Almost every moment we experience becomes a rehearsal in preparation
for the times to come.

Adapted from the DVD presentation *Wedlocked* by John Branyan. You can find
out more about John and his humorous takes on life, love, and marriage at
www.JohnBranyan.com.

6

Can You Hear Me Now?

Len Woods

Len and his wife, Cindi, discovered that we often influence others the most when we have no idea that they are observing us. The way we handle stressful moments can be an eye-opening event for those who watch our lives.

As ministers to college students, my wife and I often had kids in our home. Actually, this was my idea, and she graciously put up with it. After all, what's a house full of kids when you've already got your hands full with a newborn in the nursery? In fact, about eight o'clock every Sunday night, a big crowd of student leaders would gather at our home to eat, hang out, and plot ministry strategy for the coming week.

One Sunday, as we were in our living room with twenty or so collegians trying to pray and plan, the nursery monitor in our kitchen came alive with the loud, sad cries of our infant son. The guys in the group began to fidget, while the girls got all dreamy-eyed and forgot about the subject at hand. The long-suffering of the group lasted about two minutes, and then the desperate wails of my firstborn became the focus of everyone's attention.

My sleep-deprived wife excused herself from the meeting. Via the monitor, the group and I could hear her faintly trying to soothe our son, singing softly to him. Sure enough, after about ten minutes he quieted down, and she rejoined our meeting.

Five minutes passed, and the wailing suddenly resumed.

"I don't know what his deal is," my wife said. "I tried to nurse him, but he just fell asleep."

"Let me try this time," I said in a patronizing, know-it-all tone. I was about to show those youngsters how a suave minister could multitask in the childcare department. And try I did. Everything I could think of. I changed his diaper—even though it wasn't wet or dirty. I held him. Patted him. Worked up a sweat doing the Fussy Baby Dance. Gave him a pacifier. Rocked him. I emptied my bag of tricks and then invented a couple on the spot. Knowing the group was waiting in the other room magnified the pressure.

> In every marriage more than a week old, there are grounds for divorce. The trick is to find, and continue to find, grounds for marriage.
>
> —Robert Anderson

Nothing worked. The baby became more and more upset, more and more agitated. I was completely out of ideas, and his crying was only intensifying. If I hadn't been anatomically challenged, I would have tried to nurse him on the spot. *What is wrong with this child?* I wondered.

Why won't he be quiet and sleep? Doesn't he know I have an important meeting going on down the hall?

Suddenly, my weary wife appeared in the darkness. "What's wrong?" she asked.

Not sure how to take the question, I fired back. "How in the world should I know?" I hissed. "I've done everything but stand on my head!"

"So what do you want?" she asked in her most exasperated tone. Clearly, she had expected I would work wonders given the pressure I was under at the moment. Well, I couldn't deal with those expectations.

"What do I want?" I responded sarcastically. "What do I want? I want Mary Poppins!" I snarled, my voice rising. "Where's Supernanny when you need her? I don't think we can get fired from this parenting job, but I'd like to look into resigning!" Clearly, I had crossed way over the line and was making matters worse. The baby seemed to sense that I was upset and decided to add his two cents at a higher decibel level.

"Oh . . . give him to me," Cindi practically had to shout. "Go back to your *stupid* meeting!"

Angry, relieved, and in full retreat, I handed our crying child to Cindi and walked huffily back into the living room. Back into an awkward silence. Back into a setting where no one would make eye contact with me. Then, as the nursery monitor came to life again with more cries, I realized the truth: We had broadcast our animated spat and parental frustration to a roomful of wide-eyed college students! So much for my tour de force as a fully functioning minister/parent.

I tiptoed into the kitchen and turned off the monitor. No explanation seemed appropriate. As I looked around the room, I knew that most of those kids would someday be in the same place. I just wished I hadn't been the one to offer a prophetic demonstration of the ups and downs of parenting.

In hindsight I like to think that was one of our most vivid and powerful ministry lessons: what *not* to do in marital conflict and child-rearing situations!

LAUGH LESSON

Someone's always listening! Someone's always watching. We may live fairly private lives, but others will eventually see the patterns that we establish. What we develop when there are only two of us will tend to continue (and be reinforced) when there are more of us! That's why laughing when things are funny, and seeing the funny when things are too serious, are valuable patterns to build into your marriage over time.

You can catch Len's sermons online, and not through the baby monitor. As the lead pastor of Christ Community Church of Ruston, Louisiana, he gets lots of practice. Go to ***www.CCCRuston.com***.

7

I'm Not OK, and Neither Is My Wife

Ken Davis

Ken has learned that not taking yourself too seriously is an important step toward a happy marriage . . . and life.

One of the first things to go when people are trying to keep up an appearance of perfection is a sense of humor. People who are trying too hard can't laugh. And they especially can't laugh at themselves. Expressing joy is difficult when you are putting out so much effort to maintain the perception of perfection. People who know they are not all they're cracked up to be find it easier to crack up! G. K. Chesterton said that angels can fly because they take themselves lightly. We are free to laugh heartily when we take ourselves lightly.

I confess. I don't expect people to laugh just because I'm funny; I really expect them to laugh because *life* is funny, and I can't help pointing out its hilarity to others. When they see the goofy things in life that I see, they laugh with me (and sometimes at me)! My only advantage is that my mind works (or twists) in such a way that I find humor just about anywhere. I believe the Creator of life has a great sense of humor—and I don't have to go much further than my own stumbling and bumbling to come up with exhibit A.

Let me give you an example of what I mean: I walk down the street and stop to laugh in front of an average place of business, a "woman's accessory store," displaying a sign in the window that proclaims, "Ears Pierced—While You Wait." Don't you just love a service for busy people who don't have time to drop off their ears for piercing? And for those on a budget, they offer, "On Wednesdays, We Pierce Ears Half Off!" Now that would be a new fashion statement! I'm sure the owner of that store wasn't trying to be funny. But she would be amazed how many people have laughed at her window sign! I forbid my daughters from going anywhere near that place!

> A woman knows all about her children. She knows about dentist appointments and romances, best friends, favorite foods, secret fears, and hopes and dreams. A man is vaguely aware of some short people living in the house.
>
> —unknown

Someone has defined humor this way: a gentle way to acknowledge human frailty. I like that definition. It's a way of saying, "I'm not OK; you're not OK; but that's OK!" None of us is OK.

Like I said, I think laughter comes from people who don't take themselves too seriously. You show me people who can't laugh, and every time I'll show you people who take themselves too seriously. This is especially true in marriage. And by the way, you show me people who take themselves too seriously, and I'll show you people who don't take God seriously enough! I mean, we can fool each other part of the time about being OK, but we can't fool God. He knows we're goofy. He sees it all. He loves us anyway. Not only did He have a big hand in making us goofy, but He knows all the silly things we do with our goofiness! He's the Author of joy because He makes it possible for us to deal with our not-OK-ness. The parts of us that are not OK because of sin He can forgive and clean up; the parts of us that are just plain goofy He finds lovable. He loves when we laugh out of joy. Laughter isn't foreign to God; it's one of His gifts to us.

I'm amazed at how difficult it is for some people to realize that God doesn't mind if we laugh in His presence. Why is it that Sunday mornings are often the most serious, most joyless times in people's lives? How many times have you found yourself on Sunday morning shouting at a child you deeply love, "You get ready for church and get ready *now*! We need to get-there-on-time-to-learn-about-the-love-of-Jesus!"

Jesus Himself got into a lot of trouble because certain people didn't think He was nearly serious enough about the Sabbath. Not only did Jesus and His disciples snack on that holy day, but He took time to bring real joy into people's lives by healing them. What do you think was the first thing people did when Jesus healed their vision and they could see for the first time? They shouted! Laughed! Responded with joy! At the very least, God wants us to enjoy ourselves as we worship Him.

My wife likes to strike a good balance when it comes to taking Sunday seriously. For example, she insists that I shower before church. And when our kids were young, she had certain rules that she wanted all of us to remember about Sunday. These were good rules. They allowed for some freedom without going overboard into mind-numbing serious-ness. Naturally, as dad, I was expected to set an example. One particu-lar Lord's Day, the woman I love came downstairs, and she had no lips. They had disappeared. Between her nose and her chin there was only a very thin line under tremendous pressure. That little vein in the side of her neck was throbbing, and it was bigger than my leg. Now, I'm not mocking her—I'm just trying to show you how the Devil tries to destroy joy! With that vein, I'm not kidding, I could take her pulse from across the room. And her left eye was twitching all over the place.

She issued a command through those thin lips. "Everybody! Come in here!" The rest of the family came into the kitchen and sat down. "I'll tell you something," she began. "I am *sick* and *tired* . . ."

I've been married thirty-five years to this woman, and I've never seen her get *just* sick. She always gets really *tired* along with sick . . .

"I'm sick and tired of children treating church like a rock concert! They don't sit still! They go to the bathroom in herds! They play little annoying games with one another—I'll tell you something! We're hav-ing a new rule around here. Whatever you have to do, you do it before we get to church. And when we get into church, you will sit down and you will . . . not . . . *move!*"

None of us moved. We couldn't even breathe. She asked, "Do you understand?"

I said, "Yes," so she turned to the children . . .

We got to church, and despite our best efforts, we were a little late. That only increased the tension. All the best seats were taken, and we had to go down near the front.

We had just gotten seated when we all had to stand for the opening hymn. I suddenly realized I had an urgent need to leave for a few minutes. Of all the days and times this should happen! . . . But I knew I had to move.

So I leaned toward my wife, and in a church whisper I said, *"Honey, I have to go."*

She turned slowly toward me, and her lips disappeared again. In a strained whisper she hissed, *"You . . . will . . . not . . . move. You know the rule!"*

I pleaded, "Yes, I know . . . but I have to go."

"If you leave," she whispered intensely, "you're going to set a bad example!"

"If I stay, I'm going to set a bad example!" I snapped.

Well, I left, and I came back as quickly as I could. It was a long hymn, and I managed to return during the last verse. I slipped into the pew just as the song ended and sat down with everyone else. I'm telling you, I could feel shards of anger moving from her toward me. They were sharp, and they were hot. You know, when you're married for a while, you don't even have to look—I could feel the signs. I was in trouble.

But being a man of God, I put my arm around my wife's shoulders and gently squeezed, in a loving sign of reconciliation. I tenderly hugged her to my side, and in return she began to dig and grind her elbow deep into my ribs. This was pure stealth because the attack was carried out below the level of the back of the pew, where no one could see. It hurt! I was shocked. After all, we were in church! Right in the middle of God's house, she was poking me in the ribs with her elbow.

Well, I'd had it. And I heard God speak to me. He'd had it too. "Rebuke this woman," He said. If you don't know church and marriage language, that means, "Tell her really nicely but firmly to quit that."

So I turned to look her in the eye and tell her to quit . . . but she wasn't my wife! In my haste, I had returned to the wrong pew. My wife was sitting right behind me. I'm pretty sure that's where the anger had been radiating from!

Well, the preacher had been observing this episode unfold. Remember, we were right down toward the front. He saw it all, and he lost his composure. I've never seen the man laugh so hard in my life. Tears began to flow down his cheeks. He pointed at me as he fought for self-control, and the people around us began to laugh too. It was contagious. My friends sitting in the church knew that I wasn't OK. And when the preacher got ahold of himself, he said, "If God can love *that* man, He can love anybody."

I sneaked a peek at the woman I loved. And I saw that very thin line where I knew lips were hiding burst into a beautiful smile. I'll tell you, when you're as not OK as I am, a loving woman with a sense of humor makes all the difference, even if she's not OK either.

LAUGH LESSON

Let's face it, everyone is "goofy." Couples need to accept and laugh at their goofiness. Taking yourselves too seriously prevents you from experiencing many other parts of the life and marriage God has planned. Lighten up!

Adapted from personal appearances by Ken Davis. You can find much more about Ken at *www.KenDavis.com*, including booking information, personal quirks, his blog, and products to buy, such as DVDs, books, and more!

8

The Man Who Will Not Let Me Sleep

Amanda Huddle

Basic survival functions like eating and sleeping take on added importance when they have to be undertaken and coordinated with another person . . . for the rest of life!

My whole life the one activity that I have really loved, the one thing that I've been really good at, is sleeping. I'll have to ask my mom what kind of baby personality I had in terms of sleeping, but it seems to me that since I started school, the one thing I could do exceptionally well was sleep. Other kids were good at math, won the science fair, could do things that involved hand-eye coordination (like soccer or tennis, both of which I tried and was miserable at). Me, I could sleep. I think I actually could win a gold medal in snoozing through my alarm, being late to school or work, and/or oversleeping. In my tender twenty-something years I've probably already set a world record without even knowing it.

In college I could easily sleep until three o'clock on a Saturday afternoon while my roommate watched a dozen episodes of *The Real*

World: Boston, and the residents of my dorm had a flag football game in the hallway. It is well known that when I am depressed about something, you can find me asleep—with the dog, of course—in my room. This is a genetic marker passed down on my mother's side. My grandmother could often be found asleep on the couch, covered from chin to ankles in the day's newspaper (another genetic marker: we must be *covered* in order to sleep properly). My mom is usually asleep in her chair with a dog on her lap by no later than 9:30 PM, especially if we're watching a movie she's never seen.

> ♥ When I woke up this morning my [wife] asked
> ♥ me, "Did you sleep good?" I said, "No, I made a few
> ♥ mistakes."
> ♥
> —Stephen Wright

Anyway, everything was going just fine with me and sleeping until I married (gasp!) *a morning person.* I realized when we were dating that it might be a problem when John knocked on my door at 6:00 AM to take me out for pancakes. Back in those days it was so *romantic* and sweet, and I let it slide because he thought I looked good in my jammies with no makeup and didn't mind being seen in public with me that way. (Sigh.) And then I came home and went right back to bed with a full stomach and a whole bed all to myself.

Then we got married. He got up between 5:30 and 7:00 AM while I got up at 9:00 at *the earliest.* This upset my new husband, who couldn't stand the hours he had to wait for me to get up so we could be together. It also bugged him that my dog, Henry, wouldn't leave his spot next to my side of the bed until I got up for the day. And so the dance began. At around 7:00, he would come in and start poking me. He would "accidentally" leave his alarm on snooze and hide in another part of the house with his headphones on. He would get the dog up on the bed and try to get *him* in on it (but we know whose side Henry was on, so that tactic was a bust).

After a few months, it was clear that *this was not going to work*. I might have had a fit of tears, screaming in tired frustration that I *need* more sleep than he does and he'd better leave me alone *or else*. For the most part he gave up and let me sleep. He accepted me for who I am. Eventually I got a job that had me up at 5:00 most mornings, and I was up before him anyway. He learned that if I didn't nap, there was crying and gnashing of teeth, and no one was happy.

But now that we're back in a position where I don't have to get up too early, old Johnny is making a reappearance every once in a while. This morning he left his alarm on snooze, again. Then when my phone rang at 8:30 AM, he came in and said loudly, "CAN YOU TALK? NO? NO, SHE CAN'T TALK RIGHT NOW. WHAT? WHAT DID YOU SAY?" And so I was up at the ungodly hour of 8:50 AM and threatening my husband that if he didn't let me sleep now that I'M NEVER HAVING KIDS WITH HIM BECAUSE WE ALL KNOW THAT BABIES DON'T SLEEP and MEN DON'T KNOW HOW TO BREAST-FEED.

Hopefully our kids will get my sleeping gene. Or else my husband better figure out how to start lactating.

LAUGH LESSON

Morning person versus night person—this is a common marriage dilemma and area of adjustment. Actually, marriage involves a series of adjustments and compromises as loving couples learn to live with each other. Learning to live and laugh with the person you married, as he or she is today and each day through the changing seasons and years, is one of the most valuable opportunities that marriage offers.

A pastor's wife, mom, and track coach, Amanda discovers humor in every aspect of her life. You can read more at her blog, *http://InsideDog.typepad.com*.

9

Let It Snow

Len Woods

Life, they say, is a journey. So is marriage. But on that journey, a number of side trips turn out to be episodes fraught with danger (and stress) and seeded with possibilities for laughter. But Len isn't sure he can always tell the difference!

Christmas 1990 loomed large on the horizon. Our firstborn was seven months old, and my wife's parents in Indianapolis were chomping at the bit to see their new grandson on his first Christmas. Obviously we *had* to go, Cindi would continue to remind me. So feeling parental and grandparental pressure (guilt), I agreed and began to make plans.

But just as we were about to depart from Louisiana early on the morning of December 23, we received news of an arctic blast bringing frigid temperatures and severe ice storms to the Midwest. Now what should we do? We weighed the options: long drive versus convenience of home; dangerous trek versus snow-free, safe streets; disappointed in-laws, guilt, frustrated wife, guilt (did I mention guilt?). We confirmed our previous decision.

For a day we waited and fretted, looking for a break in the weather.

We paced. Pondered travel advisories. Monitored the Weather Channel. Finally on Christmas Eve, at about one in the afternoon (after some heated discussion, which I figured could melt any snow we might encounter), we threw caution to the wind and suitcases into the car and headed north. No way a little white stuff was going to ruin *our* holidays. With bravado and a Toyota packed full of baby paraphernalia, we set out on the twelve-hour trek north.

What happened next was like something out of a Stephen King novel.

Winter decided to detour south. Nobody was on the road, including—at times—us. In some places we could barely *see* the road. Even with our Camry heater blowing full blast, ice was forming on the *inside* of our car windows. At about Little Rock, Arkansas, I began having visions of being the subject of a *Dateline* episode. (I'd love to include our dialogue here, but I'm not sure we were on speaking terms . . . or I've totally suppressed that part of this adventure.)

We crunched and slid our way up the interstate as our restless, fussy baby squalled to be nursed. We passed countless abandoned vehicles— no doubt filled with frozen cadavers—stuck in roadside snow drifts. Darkness descended. In the dashboard light, my breath became the Ghost of Christmas Not-to-Be. I clenched the wheel even harder and slowed to 40 to 45 mph. I could feel the blood surging through the protruding veins in my temples. I felt like Mel Gibson in a wintry sequel of *The Road Warrior* and began to check my rearview mirror for roving bands of bloodthirsty Vandals. But we were the only pair of headlights in sight for thirty to forty-five minutes at a time.

By 3:00 AM we were inching our way across the Illinois–Indiana line. By 5:30 in the dim light of day—praise God, thank You, Jesus, hallelujah!—we were thawing out, physically and relationally, in my in-laws' home and looking for a space to get horizontal.

We were bleary and weary, but Christmas Day was fine. Delightful days followed. Then, on December 29 the flu hit. With a vengeance. Each day, another family member would succumb. Fever. Delirium. I spent my birthday projectile vomiting—a great way to impress the in-laws. I would have summoned Dr. Kevorkian, but I was too weak to make it to the phone. I settled for a trip to the local ER to be rehydrated via IV. Under the influence of painkillers, I tried (so I'm told) to convince the healthcare workers on duty that I was the president of Nicaragua. I then proceeded to perform a couple of numbers from *Fiddler on the Roof.*

> At our wedding rehearsal, when the minister said,
> "For better or worse, richer or poorer, in sickness
> or in health," Gail responded, "I'll take better, rich,
> and healthy." The minister reminded us that it
> wasn't multiple choice!
>
> —Dave Veerman

Seven days and about seven cases of Gatorade later, we were piling back into the car for the trip home. Too weak to make the 750-mile trip in one day, we stopped at a motel to rest. Just in time to see my beloved New Orleans Saints play only their second play-off game ever. Surely they would redeem my miserable vacation break, right? Wrong. The Saints turned back into the "Ain'ts," losing to the Chicago Bears 16–6.

Thoroughly disgusted and feeling sick to my stomach all over again, I disappeared into the bathroom. As I flushed the commode, my stylish new Seiko watch (a Christmas gift!) slid off my wrist, splashed into the swirling water, and disappeared from view.

"NO!" I screamed. "No WAY!"

"What's wrong?" my startled wife yelled as she came running.

Sputtering and waving my arms, I told her what had happened. She shook her head in disbelief.

"That sums up this trip perfectly," I concluded. *"Two weeks straight down the toilet!"* This was not one of my better moments as a loving husband.

We've had lots of pleasant trips and vacations since then. But none more memorable. And, upon further review, none that can make us laugh like that one.

LAUGH LESSON

It's always important to avoid the phrase "this is as bad as it gets," because that's when something worse happens. Sometimes, things get so bad that they cross the fine line into funny. The choice to cry is, in an odd way, right next to the choice to laugh. Unfortunately, sometimes we blame each other for conditions that are out of our control—weather, the economy, political winds, sickness. That's when we need to pray, cut each other some grace, and ask, "Is there any possibility that someday, a long time from now, we'll look back on today and laugh?" The question just might get things turned around in the right direction. And remember, God is good, all the time!

Len has stayed in the South and usually ventures north only in the summer.

He is the lead pastor at Christ Community Church in Ruston, Louisiana.

For more on the church and Len (you can even listen to his sermons), visit *www.CCCRuston.com*.

10

The Ninety-Five Irritations

Phil Callaway

A wise and well-timed comment turned out to be one of those lasting lessons that slightly alter everything that comes after. Phil got some unexpected but priceless wisdom before marriage that has borne repeated good fruit. That piece of wisdom was about turning annoyances around.

Six months before my wedding day, an elderly friend tapped my shoulder in the post office and offered me some free advice. "Ramona's a lovely girl," he said. "She deserves a good husband. Marry her before she finds one." Then he whispered a curious thing: "You want a happy marriage?"

Of course I did.

"When the things that attracted you to her start to drive you apart," he said, smiling, "find a way to reverse the process."

I've been thinking about his advice for many years, and it's starting to make sense. When Ramona and I were dating, I loved the way she took life slowly. She taught me to stop and taste the strawberries. But three months after our honeymoon, as I waited in the car, resisting the urge to honk, I knew exactly what he meant.

At one point I had considered nailing a list of ninety-five irritations to the bathroom door, something Martin Luther may have done to his wife. Only four came to mind:

1. **Your sense of humor is warped.** You thought the funniest thing I did this week was hit my head on a cupboard door. You laughed. That was not funny. Please do not laugh when you read this.

2. **You are kind to telemarketers.**

3. **My wool sweater is missing.** The one I got for my seventeenth birthday. I suspect it may have gone the way of my favorite broken-in flannel shirt—the one with that endearing campfire spark hole. That one has been AWOL for several months too.

4. **I love to be on time. You do not.** Meet me in the living room at 8:00 PM sharp, and we'll talk about this.

Thankfully, I refrained from posting the list and considered the elderly man's advice to "reverse the process." Now, after twenty-five years of marriage, I've learned that if my wife and I were the same, we'd be in trouble. If we kept all my wool sweaters, we'd need thirteen U-Hauls each time we moved.

Her kindness to telemarketers is the same kindness that first drew me to her. Thankfully, it has tempered with time. She now offers a polite "No, thanks" followed by a click. Or she says, "Here, I'll let you talk to my husband." I've asked her to meet me in the living room at 8:00 PM sharp to talk about this.

I do know I'm going to have to come up with another word for "sharp" when I'm talking with my wife about our schedule. I'm sure if I asked her, "Honey, how do you spell *sharp*?" she would smile sweetly and answer, "*s-u-g-g-e-s-t-i-o-n*."

♥

Speaking of talking, my wife got me a GPS for Christmas. It's so cool. Guys can now have a woman in their cars telling them what to do! They no longer have to stop and ask for directions. You know why the children of Israel wandered in the wilderness for forty years? Moses had no GPS and he refused to ask his wife for directions.

Sometimes this new arrangement gets confusing, though. If both your wife and the GPS are talking, you're not sure who's saying what. "Turn left in five hundred yards. Stop fiddling with the CD player. Turn left in two hundred yards. Slow down, honey. See, you missed your turn. Recalculating. Quit picking your nose. I told you so."

This is the closest I will ever come to polygamy: two women in my car giving me nonstop instructions. It presents a dilemma for us married guys. What if your wife and the GPS lady disagree? Who are you gonna listen to? You wanna be a happily married guy, so you listen to your wife. As a result, a GPS unit may be an unnecessary accessory. That's why you'll find these things in ditches everywhere. Don't buy one this Christmas. Find a ditch somewhere and load up.

LAUGH LESSON

Very few things about the relationship we call marriage are mechanical or mathematical. We don't figure things out one day and then sail smoothly through the rest of marriage. Every day is a new teachable moment. If we are really learning anything, we're learning to adapt better to what won't change or to what changes at a moment's notice!

Phil Callaway and his wife, Ramona, recently celebrated their twenty-fifth wedding anniversary. Phil was on time, but got lost twice on the way to the restaurant. For info on Phil's latest books, free laughs, inspiring articles, and complimentary expired fruitcake, visit *www.LaughAgain.org*.

11

Inventing Blackened Chicken

Tom Burggraf

"Memories . . . of the way we were," so the song goes. The shared moments in your marriage mean you now can wink at each other because something has jogged that memory, and only the two of you understand. Tom and his wife, Cherie, shared an unforgettable meal early in their marriage . . .

You may have been duped into thinking that Emeril Lagasse or some other well-known Cajun chef invented the popular dish blackened chicken. Not so. My wife, Cherie, and I did, albeit unintentionally. The site was not some hoity-toity Food Network test kitchen wrapped in more stainless steel than a Boeing 747, but a humble, homemade, station-wagon-size, brick barbecue pit in the backyard of our first home in San Antonio. More on that in a minute.

Cherie and I had been married for four years and had just bought our first starter home. I call it a "starter" because it was the start of many things: life with a hair-loss-inducing mortgage; learning how to shimmy around a king-size bed in a refrigerator-box-size bedroom; and attempting home repairs following a previous owner, whose apparent solution to every fix-it problem was shims made from broken paneling, five tubes of liquid nails, a sheet of one-quarter-inch-thick vinyl wall-paper with pastel flowers the size of your head, and, of course, duct tape.

You can imagine that escaping to the great outdoors (referring to our driveway pad shadowed by a pecan tree that produced nuts so inedible the squirrels suffered intestinal distress) was both a priority and a sanctuary. The one item that worked even better than we could imagine or manage was our aforementioned homemade, station-wagon-size, brick barbecue pit.

This was not your ordinary homemade, station-wagon-size, brick barbecue pit, however. Judging from its size and the structural integrity of the house, I believe the original owner borrowed the bricks from several load-bearing walls to create this masterpiece. Unlike any grill in North America, it was truly "barbecue meets nuclear reactor." You could drive a herd of cattle into this contraption and cook them medium-rare before they could cry "moo." The aerodynamics of this barbecue pit were such that it transformed any fuel, such as wood (or paneling shims, if you will) or charcoal, into a raging firestorm quicker than you can say, "How do I look with no eyebrows?" These qualities had earned our barbecue pit the nickname "The Mouth of Hell." I am convinced that if we could harness its energy, we could provide power to the state of Rhode Island.

Our budget was tight, but Cherie and I had one special indulgence that we allowed ourselves—a Sunday afternoon barbecue. We were going without so many things that this was an important luxury that helped give us a needed escape from the seemingly constant struggles of living in our starter home. Chicken was the least expensive option at the grocery, and barbecue sauce covers a multitude of grilling sins. So, chicken it was. *Was* is the important word here.

At first, we tried marinating the chicken, but we learned quickly that marinades, when exposed to apocalypse-level heat, have lighter-fluid-like qualities and can be very dangerous. So we rinsed the chicken and hatched a strategy to cook it while retaining hands with which to eat it.

Here's how it worked: I was dressed in a football helmet, oven mitts, and wet bath towels wrapped from wrist to shoulder. In my hand was a long-handled fork. Cherie stood a safe distance behind me holding the garden hose with spray nozzle.

With the strike of a kitchen match, the inferno was raging. The flames jumped out toward me, but my suit held firm. I stabbed a raw piece of chicken, thrust it into the blaze, and watched it spontaneously combust. I shouted over the roar of the fire for Cherie to call it when she thought the meat was cooked. I received her signal, backed up, and held the burning bird high above my head as Cherie quickly shot it with the hose, dousing the flames and creating an impressive billow of steam. This was repeated until all four pieces of chicken were cooked.

When we brought the plate into the kitchen, we had four unrecognizable steaming blobs that looked as if four meteorites had landed on the plate. This was to be our special dinner. Cherie's eyes filled with tears, and we held each other. I would not be paid again until Tuesday, and we had spent the rest of our food budget on the chicken. I didn't want to see her upset. Her body was shaking now, although not with sobs but with laughter.

"Your arms wrapped in those wet towels are getting me soaked!" she said. "And you look ridiculous. If we can make a home in this house, I know I can make a meal out of this chicken." She was right.

Cherie chipped off the burnt skin, shaved off the charred meat on the outside, and sculpted from it shapes that were recognizable as food.

I got the salad and corn ready, and we sat down at our mismatched dinette with a huge pitcher of iced tea (to rehydrate us after taking the heat from the cooking process). We lingered over our dinner, joking about how good it tasted as we chewed . . . and chewed . . . and chewed. We were like sweethearts on our first Valentine's Day. And we wouldn't have changed a thing.

Many years have passed since that starter home, and since then I have been able to obtain a grill that does not resemble the mouth of Hades and can do everything but cut and serve the meat. But I wonder if we'll ever have a meal together that provides us more joy than that Sunday afternoon when we invented blackened chicken.

LAUGH LESSON

You can bet that any time Tom and Cherie go to a restaurant that serves blackened chicken, they look over the tops of their menus and smile at each other—both remembering the same day, the same incident, the same incendiary grill. This is what makes memories. Many times even a small investment, such as chicken for a Sunday afternoon barbecue, makes for a strong marriage and the opportunity to laugh at a special memory.

Tom is bivocational in Gunnison, Colorado. That is, he works for the local university (Western State College of Colorado) and pastors Bethany Baptist Church. For more on Tom and the church, visit *www.GunnisonBethany.com.*

12

Marriage License

John Branyan

John Branyan has apparently spent way too much time in DMV offices over the years, but he has made some interesting observations about the license to marry.

Have you noticed that you have to get your driver's license renewed every few years . . . but you don't have to get your marriage license renewed—ever! Now isn't that interesting?

I mean, you would think there would at least be some kind of an eye test to make sure you can still see well enough to be married! They would have you look through the ugly machine with the binocular eyepieces—"All right, Mr. Branyan, can you see your socks on the floor?" Or, for the written test you would have to use a pencil, but it would be up to you to find one. I'd be in big trouble right there. I can go looking in a room for days and find nothing; my wife can make a brief visit to the same room and find two pencils, a pen, and a box of crayons . . . all in the seat cushions. I just know my wife could pass the marriage-license test with flying colors—but I'd be signed up for remedial marital training every time!

I've known only one guy in my whole life who could even try to keep up with the woman in his life when it came to conversations and stuff. That was Great-Grandfather Frank. He and Great-Grandmother Mamie had this little thing that they worked out, almost like a routine. Mamie would say things to us boys like, "Boys, don't stick your fingers in your nose. Don't do that!"

Great-Grandpa Frank would be hovering behind us and ask, "If you're not supposed to put your fingers in your nose, how come they fit?" He sure had a fine sense for the unanswerable argument!

I've been married for twenty-one years—to the same person! I think the secret to a long-term relationship is flexibility, adaptation. You've got to learn to bend with the wind . . . or it will knock you flat! That's because marriage is always in a state of flux; it's always changing. After twenty-one years, she's not the same girl I married. The relationship is a lot more *intense*. She asks me questions. Questions that I don't know the answers to . . . because they are questions that no man has ever known the answers to! These are deep, probing, impossible questions. Questions like, "What are you thinking?"

♥ **Like good wine, marriage gets better with age—**
♥ **once you learn to keep a cork in it.**
♥
—Gene Perret

I'm a guy. I'm thinking nothing. Zero, zip, zilch—nada. She's a girl—girls cannot think nothing! That never happens. Even when her mind is blank, there are billions of calculations going on, angles being considered, thoughts being processed and organized, colors being coordinated. She's like a 352-terabyte file-server computer; I'm like that little solar powered calculator that comes free in a cereal box.

And I still spend time with other guys. Me and the guys go out—we talk. Never once have I ever said, "Hey, Al, what are you thinking?" 'Cause I don't care. Plus, he's a guy. I know what he's thinking—nothing.

♥

Has this ever happened to you? Saturday morning I'm minding my own business. On my way out to mow the yard, or something, she stops me dead in my tracks, kind of like a traffic officer, but without the whistle. "Are you going to wear *that* outside?"

I am stunned. "I'm just going to mow. What's the big deal?"

"Look at your shirt! Look at those pants! And look at those socks! I don't want the neighbors to see you looking like that!"

Sunday morning I come out the same door going to church, and she stops me again for an appraisal of her outfit. She throws in a twirl for effect. "OK, sweetheart. How do I look?"

"Why are you asking me? I'm not even qualified to dress myself!"

Men are not qualified to do so many things, yet tasks continue to fall to us. For centuries they have been left to us. We don't know how to do them—you know, *fix* things. The repair gene is supposed to be innate. "Look, John, all our stuff, everything around the house—it's all broken, busted, not working . . . so fix it."

I know only one electronic repair maneuver—a firm hit on the side of the offending piece of machinery. Broken VCR? Open-handed slap on the side. Microwave's on the fritz? Pow! Take that! In dire cases I might use a tool to assist me—perhaps a hammer or some other tool that will serve as a hammer in my hands. If it's a tall appliance like a refrigerator or freezer, some kicking might be involved. I'm convinced that in the first year of medical school, they have to teach all the male doctors not to walk in the room and say, "Hi, how do you feel, Mr. Smith? Are you still sick?" Pow! "There—a nice blow to the side of the head ought to have you up and running in no time."

My wife also wants me to be prepared to respond in unnatural ways. For example, she expects to borrow things from me that I never have— like tissue. "I've got a little sniffle, honey. Can I borrow a tissue?" The tone in her voice and the look on her face tell me she really expects that I will have such things at hand. But no, I don't carry Kleenex! For a guy, carrying Kleenex and wearing long sleeves is redundant. Why carry a onetime use thing like Kleenex when long sleeves were clearly meant to multitask.

Once every millennium or so, just like clockwork, my wife will assign me a project that actually falls within my tiny little sphere of competence. And I get so excited because I can finally demonstrate to her that I'm not completely without purpose. She'll say, "Sweetheart, I've got a little headache. That's why my eyes are crossed right now. Would you be a dear and get me an aspirin?"

I think, *Yes! I can get you an aspirin! I know what those are . . . I know where they are! I'll make you proud, and you'll be glad you married me!* And I say, "Right away, honey." I run down the hall to the bathroom, fling open the medicine cabinet, and reach for the aspirin—in the child-resistant bottle sitting there on the shelf. What follows is a humiliating demonstration of frustration as I end up on the floor trying to get that little red cap off the container. Utterly defeated, I return to the living room with the unopened bottle. "Here, honey." She opens it without even breaking a sweat.

I can't even read my own temperature when I don't feel well. Trying to read that glass thermometer is like looking into a crystal ball. I'm just not gifted that way. I hand it to her and she says, "This is the baby thermometer. Do you know where this has been?" I'm trying to control my gag reflex as I gargle with gallons of mouthwash.

I can't fix things. And I can't operate . . . Tupperware. Before I can get those airtight covers on, everything that was in the container is down my front. I can't master Ziploc bags. My wife can explain the science involved. "See, honey, when you join the blue stripe with the yellow stripe, it makes a green stripe—that's how you know it's sealed!" Easy for her to say. She has more experience with zippers. I mean she's got zippers that zip up in the back of her dresses. What's that for? To make it more challenging? All my zippers are in the front . . . and I still forget to close them. Come to think of it, if I had to qualify for a license for everyday living, I'd be in big trouble!

LAUGH LESSON

All married couples are *amateurs* at the task of being married to each other. So we all need on-the-job training as we learn about ourselves, our spouses, and the dynamic and creative experience of living and relating together. And we're sure to have numerous chuckles, guffaws, and belly laughs along the way as we recognize our foibles and narrowsightedness. But "love covers over a multitude of sins" (1 Peter 4:8), and the willingness to laugh (particularly at yourself) keeps the door open to all that life has to offer.

Adapted from DVD presentation *Wedlocked* by John Branyan. You can find out more about John's adventures and unique take on life at ***www.John Branyan.com***.

Finding Our Way

Chonda Pierce

The truism that men won't ask for directions hides a deeper truism: Men really don't want to admit they need direction! Some of the ways we try to compensate for this serious shortcoming lead to not-so-serious results.

I've been married to David for twenty-six years now. I've known him for more than thirty. We first met in high school. That's fifteen cars, five houses, two children, twenty-something dogs, and seven cats ago. It was also before cell phones and GPS gadgets, both of which have at times tested our love but ultimately glued us together.

Back in high school, we lived in a small town with a main street and a couple of offshoots. There was no way to get lost. But then again, I don't think owning a GPS is about not getting lost. I believe if the technology had been around then, David would have owned a GPS. He's a direction taker—at least from anyone besides me. Thirty years ago he'd have loved to have an electronic box fastened to his windshield with a suction cup with an Australian-accented hoochie mama instructing him to turn "riiiight" at the "liiiight."

We took a road trip from Tennessee to Louisiana not long ago. David

punched the ending address into the GPS, and we took off. I sensed
that we were in trouble when Miss Hoochie had us exit the interstate
somewhere just south of Memphis—a long way from Shreveport.

We drove past casinos in Mississippi, passed through towns with
populations less than the number of women in the men's room at any
Women of Faith conference.

"Are you sure—" I started, but David doesn't like for his GPS to be
second-guessed.

> ♥ If Laurie, Linda, Michelle, and Liz go out for lunch,
> ♥ they will call each other Laurie, Linda, Michelle,
> ♥ and Liz. If Mark, Juan, Franklin, and Paul go out,
> ♥ they will affectionately refer to each other as
> ♥ Fat Boy, Godzilla, Peanut Head, and Snappy.
>
> —unknown

"Hey, maybe she knows a shortcut," he snapped back.

She?

"I'm just saying that all these signs about alligator sandwiches are
starting to make me hungry."

David sat up straighter. He waved a hand in the direction of the
GPS. "Punch the little food icon," he said. "She'll tell you every eating
place that's nearby."

I made a move for the GPS, but David stopped me. "Not yet," he
said, a protective hand hovering above Hoochie Mama's home. "Wait
until we get to a good long straight stretch. Don't want to miss a turn."

There are no good long straight stretches through Mississippi . . . or

Arkansas . . . or the northern part of Louisiana. At one point we came upon some road construction and wound up in a neighborhood with stop signs every block. "Didn't we pass by that house before?" I asked. Hoochie Mama kept saying, "Go zero point one mile and then take a riiiight." I've never seen David follow directions so heartily. "We just made a circle," I said as we passed a little blue house with a tractor in the front yard and a Doberman chained to the front tire.

"That's not the same Doberman," David said. He kept hanging right. Hoochie Mama kept directing. The interstate was far, far away.

"Can we get an alligator burger now?" I asked. Somehow, some-way—despite the plaintive "recalculating route" of Hoochie Mama—we found a gas station that served greasy burgers and boiled peanuts. They also sold maps. I bought one and spread it out on the front seat.

David seemed nervous. "I'm sure if we just give her a bit more time—"

"Look," I said, stabbing a finger at the map. "That big blue line is the interstate. We're right here. Go up to this yellow line here," I traced the highway with my finger, "turn right on this green line, and we're there."

"Turn which way?"

"Right," I said. David waited. "Okay," I said. "Drive up this yellow road and then turn riiight at the green road. Then take a riiight up the raaamp to the blue road." To keep the map from sliding around, I used the GPS to hold it in place. I might have even gotten a bit of alligator grease on her—I mean, *it*.

LAUGH LESSON

Marriage includes the discovery of one another's shortcomings. You may find out that your mate is simply incapable of performing certain tasks, with an appalling level of incompetence. Your spouse may even be will-ing to try to learn, but, alas, he or she is not able to accomplish what you think should come naturally . . . except, of course, for those jobs that *you* can't do. (Funny, isn't it, how we excuse ourselves?) Sometimes just going with the flow can lead to the greatest fun, as long as neither of you is tak-ing matters too seriously.

Adapted from the life of Chonda and David Pierce. Find out more about them and Chonda's comedy at ***www.chonda.org***.

14

Technical Difficulties

Chonda Pierce

After having been single, newly married couples can find the adjustment of asking for help and working together a bit awkward. But having a helper is a gift, especially when the husband or wife needs help solving a problem that he or she caused.

Ladies, here's something that is certain: If you own a cell phone . . . one day you will drop it into the lake.

Most likely it will bounce off the dock—two, three times, all in super slow motion—before plopping into the still, deep waters. Then you will stare at that spot, where the water ripples, thinking: *Maybe it floats.* But it won't float, so you will do the best you can with the tools you have: You'll ask your husband to go after it. "Come on," you'll tell him, "it's a search and rescue mission."

My husband, David, is a scuba diver, so he jumped in right away, only to pop right back up, spitting and coughing up water. "Forgot I don't have an air tank," he said. He hung on the dock for a few moments—just breathing—and all the time my phone was drowning.

Finally, he took one last deep breath, went under, and began poking around on the bottom, about eight feet down. My phone wears a hot pink cover, so I figured it should be easy to spot down there. Suddenly I had a great idea: I took *his* phone and called *mine*, thinking it might just ring and the ringing could lead him to it. You know, like sonar waves help dolphins find those underwater mines. After some long seconds he came up without my phone and said we needed to let the mud settle, because he couldn't see a thing down there. In the meantime I used his phone again to change my voice mail: "I can't talk to you right now because I'm at the bottom of the lake!" Maybe you called me sometime around then and wondered what that was all about. That's what that was all about.

♥ **Men wake up as good-looking as when they**
♥ **went to bed. Women somehow deteriorate during**
♥ **the night.**
♥
                                                        —unknown

David took this downtime to retrieve his diver's mask. He got his snorkel, too, but I reminded him that unless it was an eight-foot snorkel, it wouldn't be of much help. He said he knew that; he was just showing me that he had one. I told him I already knew that he had one. He said he thought that I did already know that. We went a couple of more rounds like that, but I won't write it all down because the repetition gets irritating. It's one of those patterns that all marriages develop. This is one of ours—who knew what and when they knew it.

Anyway, he tossed the snorkel back onto the bank, fitted his mask over his eyes, and dove to the bottom of the lake for my phone. Topside

I waited, prayed, and speed-dialed my number—just in case. Then, like that scary guy in *Friday the 13th* who shoots up out of the water knife first, up comes David waggling the phone above his head. Whether he needed it or not, I gave him a quick mouth-to-mouth moment. He was my hero and deserved to be treated as such. As long as he didn't let it go to his head.

Ladies, when you get your phone back from the bottom of the lake, first you will shake it like a saltshaker. Water will glug out. Then you will blow into all the cracks and seams and around the numbers. Water will spray you in the face. Then you're going to push the On button and put it to your ear to see if you can hear anything. Meanwhile, your husband, when he's finished spitting and gasping for air, will say something like "I'm going to get you one of those trucker chains for Christmas so you can hook it to that phone and not let this happen again." I can't think of a single outfit that goes well with a long, dangling chain attached to my phone. Looks like I'm about to set another fashion trend.

♥

The Mission: Missing Cell Phone was accomplished—together. But often we don't always work so well side by side. Sometimes we even scare each other—and we don't mean to! I can be working in the kitchen, David can turn a corner, and "AHHH!" a soup spoon will go flying through the air from my hand. "Why do you do that?" I'll say.

"Do what? Walk through my own house? You don't recognize me?"

"Just try to make some noise before you step into a room like that."

"What kind of noise?"

"I don't know. Sing, whistle. Just let me know you're on your way before you get there."

It's gotten so bad lately that I can actually watch him walk into the closet, and if he's in there for more than a minute, when he comes out, I'll jump and say, "Why do you do that?" And he'll say, "What? I can't walk through my own house?" This could go on like this all day. And my real fear is that it could go on for years to come. So, not long ago we tried something different. David would walk through the house saying things like, "Walking down the hallway of my own house! Turning the corner and taking that hallway that leads to the kitchen! Stopping off for a drink in the guest restroom! About to make a sudden appearance in the doorway . . ."

"You don't have to sound like a GPS, you know," I tell the smart aleck. I should know by now that rebukes are received as encouragement.

"Turning riiiight into the den . . . in three steps."

It was just then, as I was coming out of the bathroom, that he turned left and spooked the dickens out of me. "AHHH!" A phone went flying through the air—from my hand—and landed in the toilet.

The room went silent. An air bubble rose to the surface and popped.

David made a U-turn and came back a minute later, with a snorkel. He already had his goggles on.

I immediately used David's phone to change my voice mail. So if you get a recording that says I can't talk now because I'm in the toilet, you'll know what that's all about.

I left before the rescue mission could begin. And I was halfway across the house when I heard David's muffled voice announce, much more loudly than really necessary, "Fishing phone out of toilet! Looking for blow-dryer . . ."

The worst thing about this whole incident is that now I know what I'm getting for Christmas.

LAUGH LESSON

Many of the humorous moments in life come out of the effort to work together. Life has a way of making those efforts dissolve into laughter. The lesson is to decide to keep working together, not only because life is better that way, but because working together won't always work out the way you and your spouse expected!

Adapted from the true-life romance of Chonda and David Pierce. Find out more about them and Chonda's comedy at *www.chonda.org*.

15

Garage Sale

Daren Streblow

Among those traits that get filed under "ways I'm different from my spouse"
is the tendency to assign very different value to the same objects. The Streblows
continue to discover this basic fact of life.

I love being married! However, conflict is always inevitable when you
have two separate minds and wills working together. This is especially
true if one person is passionate about an idea and the other isn't. My
wife gets very excited about having garage sales. She considers hosting a
garage sale her opportunity to get rid of everything in the house that
she doesn't want. It turns out most of that stuff is mine.

Now, I don't mind cleaning house every now and again. I even think
the whole garage sale idea is great. I mean, why put your garbage in
Hefty bags and throw it in a Dumpster when you can sell it to strangers?
But the problem is the stuff my wife wants to get rid of is *not* garbage—
it's my collection of treasures.

My wife doesn't feel the same connection to my prized possessions
as I do, which is where the conflict comes in. We see things differently.

Where she sees the flaws, I see great beauty. For example, she would want to sell my old Operation game. Her argument is, "It's missing that light-up buzzer nose!" Well, to me, that makes the game easier to play!

Or she might want to get rid of my G.I. Joe action figure. Can you believe that? Not only is this a collector's item, but it has features not seen in today's electronic toys. It has a lever on the back of the head that makes the eyes move back and forth. It's wonderful! But my wife would point out the negative aspect, like, "This army doll of yours is missing its body from the neck down." Granted. But don't forget that in battle, there is nothing more intimidating than a floating head coming at you. And besides, you shouldn't underestimate short people.

> ♥ A woman has the last word in any argument.
> ♥ Anything a man says after that is the beginning
> ♥ of a new argument.
> ♥
> —unknown

The biggest conflicts over potential garage sale items have involved my favorite stuffed animal and best friend growing up—Jo Jo the Monkey. Jo Jo has seen better years, but he is my friend and he belongs under my roof. My wife's desire to sell a family member is unconscionable and sparks an intense argument. We always choose our words carefully. She will use words like "musty" and "smelly" and "juvenile." I will use words like "heartless" and "cruel" and "Jezebel." Then she will say "couch," and I will usually surrender immediately.

After my wife collects all the things she wants to sell, the struggle turns to garage salers themselves. These are not normal people. They are hard to deal with. I always hope no one will show up at the garage sale, but the whole world shows up at a garage sale! And not just our world! The behavior suggests they could be beings from other planets.

Garage salers come in fast, and you have to be ready for them, or unexpected tragedy will occur. Like, someone will take the concrete steps in front of your house and leave fifty cents.

Some of the people are rude, too, and you have to know how to deal with them. Sometimes it just takes some effort on your part to educate them. For example, someone will pick up Jo Jo the Monkey by the scruff of his soft neck, hold him up high, and ask me, "How much for this thing?"

"Thing? Madam, that thing you are holding was my best friend in the world. He was my childhood friend during all the hard times, like head lice, and pink eye, and the original swine flu, and that mysterious bacterial . . ." By this time, the rude person has quickly put down Jo Jo and makes great speed out of the crowded garage, tripping over the hole in the ground that used to be my fifty-cent concrete steps.

Unfortunately, my wife is very good at hosting a garage sale, and we typically sell all of our "treasures." After three days of exhaustion and conflict, we will have made a total of ten dollars. My wife will usually sense that I'm not over the whole experience and will say to me, "Take the ten dollars." At this point, the best thing to do is take the revenue, go to some other garage sale, and buy all my stuff back. Total cost $1.50: priceless.

LAUGH LESSON

The concept of "what's yours is mine and what's mine is yours" can lead to some interesting conversations. Healthy marriages recognize the freedom of spouses to be different from each other but also remember that at the wedding both pledged, "I will." The challenge is to put both of those "wills" together.

Adapted from the comedic stylings of Daren Streblow. For more laughs and insights on married life and beyond, check out *www.DarenStreblow.com*.

16

Wait Until Next Year!

Dave Veerman

After years of marriage, grown children, and accumulating grandchildren, Dave and his wife, Gail, still like to say, in many ways, that the best is yet to come!

I'm not a hundred years old. I mention that only because it means the Chicago Cubs have not won the World Series in my lifetime. I mention that only because I'm a die-hard Cubs fan, so I've spent much of my life in frustration. I mention that only because this turned out to be a significant surprise to my bride.

Oh sure, Gail knew I was into sports. I had played college football and starred (my description, not hers) in the YMCA basketball league. I even had broken my nose playing in an all-star flag football game the day after I proposed. (To this day she insists she was a victim of "bait and switch"—after all, I was perfectly healthy with a straight nose when she accepted!) But the *real* meaning of sports to me came as a shock to her. The fact that I would channel surf, looking for signs of athletes chasing, hitting, or throwing a ball; relive the latest "game of the century," play by detailed play; purchase sports memorabilia suitable for hanging—all big surprises.

Gail's shock and subsequent adjustment reminds me of engaged couples I have met and counseled. I submit that the most difficult counseling appointment is with a couple in love—*before* the wedding. They listen intently to my words of wisdom, nodding and hmm-hmming at the appropriate moments. They even agree when I say something like "Marriage can be difficult and painful at times."

"Yes, we understand," they respond in their naïveté, with dreamy glazed-over eyes, awash in idealism.

And I want to grab the guy by the shirt, pull him close, and whisper tensely through gritted teeth, "No . . . you . . . don't . . . understand! You . . . have . . . no . . . idea!"

But I digress. Gail and I both thought we knew what we were getting into in marriage and figured we could work through the minor bumps and conflicts and differences between us with ease. Not so fast, basketball breath! To this day (after decades of marriage), Gail can't understand why I'd rather watch the Cubs load the bases with no one out *and not score a single run* and then *blow the game in the ninth with a high-paid closer who can't close* and yell at the TV—instead of watching *Designed to Sell* or *What Not to Wear* or *Divine Design* or something like that (she's an interior designer, can you tell?) on one of the high-numbered cable channels.

Yes, I'm into sports, and that stinks when you live in Chicago, where the championships are few and far between (except for the Bulls in the 1990s). And did I mention that we lived just outside of New Orleans for seven years? When we got there, the city had two teams, and one of them relocated. So we were stuck with the New Orleans Saints (the

"Ain'ts"). And, yes, I can talk your ears off with theories and facts and stacks of stats about my favorite teams. Are you sure love isn't spelled E-S-P-N? And I know God is in control, that He cares about me, that He has blessed me beyond belief, and that in His grand plan, one game is virtually meaningless, *but the loss still ruins my day*. So, yes, Gail is married to a continually frustrated sports fan (poor girl)—I mean, a hundred years of futility!

> ♥ **A woman marries a man expecting he will**
> ♥ **change, but he doesn't. A man marries a woman**
> ♥ **expecting that she won't change, and she does.**
> ♥
> —unknown

So how have we made our marriage work through this conflict of interests?

- More than one TV, so we can watch in different rooms when we need to.
- More than one child, so one can follow in Gail's footsteps and one in mine.
- More than one argument, where I've learned to admit, from time to time, that Gail is right about my sports obsession being out of control, my idol.

We have lots of other differences that surfaced after the honeymoon. For example, I thought that "a man's home is his castle." I quickly learned that in most marriages the only parts of the "castle" in the man's domain are the basement and the garage—in my case, a *part* of the basement and a *corner* of the garage. And Gail discovered my unique keen powers of observation, like when I glanced around the living room and remarked, "Hey, a new couch!" And she had to explain that we'd had it for two years.

Other significant differences emerged in sleeping habits, cleaning skills, clothing preferences (colors have to match?), spending priorities, conflict-resolution approaches (one of us gets it all out—I won't say who), storage areas (what's wrong with the top of my desk?), and my favorite: knowing when a piece of clothing should be washed, donated, or discarded! But we can't resolve those issues in separate rooms.

And we have to resolve them because, like the Cubs, I don't want to strike out on my own.

LAUGH LESSON

Due diligence in getting to know your fiancé before marriage doesn't mean there won't be surprises—on both sides. What you need to really know about your intended is the content of his or her character. The myriad of unique traits—both endearing and dreary—will combine to make marriage an interesting experience. It's not about knowing everything; it's about knowing—and loving—the most important things.

Dave is co-owner and chief creative officer (whatever that means) of The Livingstone Corporation. He has also played his nose in venues around the world. For more on Livingstone (not Dave, so much), go to ***www.Living stoneCorp.com***.

17

I Married Above Myself

David Dean

Marriages grow into greatness. The longest-lasting satisfactions in marriage come not only from what you can do for your spouse, but also from the delight of learning to do things together.

I often ask my mixed audiences, "How many of you men feel like you married above yourselves?"

About half of them admit the truth. The other half confer with their wives in fear, asking, "I don't know . . . did I, dear?" Most of them look as if their wives haven't let them state an opinion in thirty years, so why start now?

Let's face it, guys, we *did* marry above ourselves. Betsy, my wife, and I have been married twenty-two years—twenty-one of them have been happy. I refer to my wife as Saint Betsy. Anybody who lives with me is a saint. My parents have always threatened that if she and I ever split, they would take her in and leave me homeless. Saint Betsy and I met on a blind date in Chicago. The couple that set us up, also mutual friends, decided to take us to a concert an hour away. Regretfully, on the way home, I fell asleep. And snored. Yeah . . . I married above myself.

Six short months after we met, we became engaged. I figured no other woman would allow me to sleep (and snore) on a date and still find me attractive.

I'll never forget all the work that went into our wedding. OK . . . all the work Saint Betsy did to prepare for the wedding. When she mentioned that we needed to register for wedding presents at our favorite stores, I suggested Dollar General. From that point on, I, like so many millions of other married men, have learned to look at my wife first for approval before I open my mouth in public. Again, I ask the question: How many of you men feel as if you've married above yourselves?

Often I'm on the road, so I am very grateful to God for all the marvelous women Saint Betsy has in her life—women to whom she can turn for help and support. I've never met those women, but I've read their names in our checkbook. There is Mary Kay, who I believe leads a Bible study—weekly. Then there's Vera Bradley who's supposed to be a sweet gal. Then there is this German girl by the name of Longaberger. No first name, so I don't know if Betsy knows her all that well.

People always ask us how we keep our marriage strong. One word: laughter. It defuses so many bombs in our home. Couples have to laugh because the alternative is death. The Bible says never go to bed angry with each other. What practical advice. Ignore it and you could very well end up with a pillow over your face in the middle of the night. It's also one of the reasons I've never owned a weapon. Which really makes no difference, since some wives tend to be impulsive, meaning the first object they can reach in the middle of an argument, they will attack you with.

As a boy, I learned two very valuable lessons about women from my own mom. Lesson no. 1: Never upset Mother while she's in the kitchen. The kitchen contains objects that can induce the most pain: wooden spoons, frying pans, and, for all-out rage, the microwave. Say something terrible to her while she is cooking and run the risk of losing your ear. So I learned to argue with Mother in public places, where she had to appear civil. Safe places, like the pew during a church service. My best friend, Mark, liked this idea too, since his mom also suffered from RGS (Rage, Grab, and Stab) syndrome. However, Mark still carries scars on the back of his arm from where his mom would twist his skin and then whisper in his ear, "Jesus may have died for you, but I'm gonna torture you. Knock it off!"

> ♥ If a woman has to choose between catching a fly
> ♥ ball and saving an infant's life, she will choose
> ♥ to save the infant's life without even considering
> ♥ if there are men on base.
>
> —Dave Barry

Lesson no. 2: Women have acute hearing. I always wanted to get the last word in while arguing with Mom. And it seemed to work best after I had turned around and walked away . . . down the block. Then I would mumble something like, "You'll never make me wear those ugly shoes." I learned that when she yelled, "What did you just say to me?" it was really a rhetorical question. She knew exactly what I had said, but she wanted to work herself up into a frenzy. Mom could hear me mumble from two counties away, which is why I always speak highly and lovingly of her to this day.

Sometimes young couples will come to Saint Betsy and me looking for advice. What is the secret, they will ask, to making a relationship work?

Here is my answer: While you are dating, spend one Saturday a month at a boat ramp. That is a magical place. It can transform loving, happy couples into Satan and his Bride. Earlier in the day, you will enjoy hours out on the lake, skiing, tubing, laughing, telling stories, kissing, and dreaming about your future. Then, when the sun begins to set and it's time to take the boat out of the water, you will find out just how strong your love really is.

Usually, the male will back the vehicle and the boat trailer ever so slowly down the ramp (which, the first few times of doing this can ruin anybody's walk with Jesus). Since the empty trailer is almost impossible to see from the driver's seat, getting it to go where you want presents a challenge that most men desperately want to meet, but few succeed at. Meanwhile, the love of his life is at the wheel of the boat that is idling slowly up to the trailer, steering as best she can. They'll probably make eye contact with each other from a distance . . . wink, wink . . . then mouth the words "I love you. Today was *fun*."

Then the bottom drops out. The merging of the boat with its trailer does not go as planned. The trailer is not deep enough in the water or the boat sways off toward another boat. The love signals and sweet nothings of a few moments ago are forgotten in the frustration of contradictory instructions. Simultaneously, both people begin screaming at the top of their lungs in front of God and other families . . . "TOO FAR RIGHT . . . NO . . . TO MY RIGHT . . . PULL IT UP . . . ME? . . . NO . . . NOW TO THE LEFT . . . I DID . . . SHUT UP . . . I'M DOING MY BEST . . . YOU COME HERE AND DO IT . . . HURRY . . . TURN LEFT . . . YOU'RE ACTING LIKE YOUR MOTHER!"

Our boat-ramp debacle occurred in our first year of marriage. We now tell couples to practice several times in the middle of the day when no one is around the landing. This skill, along with wallpapering, is definitely fraught with danger for a young couple who approaches it with judgment clouded by romance. But get these things right, and lots of others things also go well. As I said . . . twenty-two years and twenty-one of them have been happy. I am a better man because of Saint Betsy.

LAUGH LESSON

Some of the simplest tasks in life hold the promise of great lessons. Tasks that require coordination and figuring out how to work together show up daily in marriage, and a wise couple laughingly expects to get it hilariously wrong many times on the way to getting it right.

For more information about the comedy of David Dean (booking info, too), go to *www.DavidPDean.com*.

18

The Glamorous Life of a Klutz

Amanda Huddle

Marriage, they say, is a great training ground for patience. They aren't kidding. Marriage will convince you that you don't have patience and then provide you with a continuous flow of opportunities to develop it.

If you've ever met me, the words *clumsy* or *emphatic* might come to mind. I've been known to fall up the stairs; say inappropriate things loudly at inappropriate times; and blame inanimate objects, the dogs, or my husband for moving my purse, my keys, or any manner of necessary items when I can't find them two seconds before I exit the house and am already late.

Therefore, it probably came as no surprise to anyone on Saturday night when I performed my latest feat of wonder. John and I were over at Lily and Troy's place for one of our many game marathons. (This week's poison was Rummikub, although lately we've been super into Skip-Bo.) The baby was in bed, and we were getting competitive. John and I started our usual smack-talk, and I thought I'd be all cool and give him the old "talk to the hand" sign . . . without looking. Of course, John was in the middle of taking a swig of coffee, and whaddaya know, I smacked the bottom of his mug, sending a wave—oh yes, it was a full cup—of decaffeinated glory all over his Rocky T-shirt and shorts. It was astounding how soaked he got. After the initial shock wore off and the floor and table and John were toweled off, we had a good laugh. Good-natured, wonderful Johnny put up with a wet T-shirt for the rest of the evening. A sassy mouth and endless patience . . . how could I *not* marry that man?

> I have learned that only two things are necessary to keep one's wife happy. First, let her think she's having her own way. And second, let her have it.
>
> —Lyndon B. Johnson

Well, you'd think I'd be done for a while after that one, wouldn't ya? Right . . .

Bright and early the next morning, Sunday, we were at church after Sunday school, chatting with John's best buddy, Monte. John was standing near the top of the stairs with a full cup of coffee and—you guessed it!—I decided to tease him about something and playfully put my arm around his neck and . . . whap! Another full cup of coffee murdered. Luckily this time it went only on his shoes (and all over the stairs).

Sometimes I try to claim to have a brain tumor so that maybe people will "understand" my klutzy, clumsy ways. No one believes it for a second. Can't blame a girl for trying.

LAUGH LESSON

Although some people are more agile than others, every spouse has clumsy moments in marriage. But those experiences teach forgiveness, patience, and grace—in short, love. And they lead to a few laughs along the way.

Amanda and John Huddle have learned to laugh together for several years now.

To read more of Amanda's amusings, see her blog: *http://InsideDog.typepad.com*.

19

Before and After the Marriage Vows

Dave Veerman

Before
He was attracted to her sparkling, outgoing
personality—the life of the party.
After
He is frustrated that she's the last one to leave . . .
church, a social, a committee meeting, an unexpected
conversation with a stranger at the store.

Before
She loved his well-toned muscles and ripped abs.
After
She can't believe he spends so much time at the gym.

♥

Before

Her hair, her makeup, her clothing—everything was just right.

After

She spends so much time in front of the mirror . . .

♥

Before

He was fiscally responsible, financially secure.

After

What a miser and cheapskate!

♥

Before

What a great conversationalist, never at a loss for words.

After

He can't break into her monologue.

♥

Before

She was attracted to him because he was the strong,
silent type—rock solid and steady.

After

He's so quiet . . . and boring!

♥

Before

What a great figure!

After

Can't we eat something besides tofu and sprouts?

Before

She thought it was great that he loved her cooking.

After

He never takes her out to eat.

Before

What a free spirit she was—exciting and uninhibited.

After

The house is a mess!

20

If It Isn't Broken,
Wait a Few Minutes

Neil Wilson

They say love is blind—apparently that applies to the walk-through of that first home. What starry-eyed couple hasn't overlooked the sagging floors in hopes that a little paint will create their love nest?

It was the best of houses; it was the worst of houses. The charm of old houses is that they're old. They look wise, lived in, and quaint. The curse of old houses is that they're old. Hiding behind that veneer of classic lines and noble history lurks a labyrinth of cracked, broken, outdated, and missing everything. Welcome to our dream house.

Warnings of disaster were everywhere—multisensory cautions. How could we overlook the fact that the house didn't smell right? Easy. Eyes can't smell, and we were mostly just looking. How could we not see that the foundation's stones were caving in? Easy. The lights in the basement didn't work—a minor, easily corrected electrical problem.

"Honey, are you sure electrical problems are easy to fix?" my lovely young wife inquired.

"I rewired a lamp in shop class in high school. Piece of cake."

Neither of us recognized the wisdom in my Sherrie's basic instinct. One step down into the inky, dank, damp well of the basement stairway, she turned around and said, "I love the house. If we buy it, don't ever ask me to go down here." Years later, she still shudders at the memory of her terrifying adventures into the pit on laundry days.

And how on earth could we miss the leaky roof? Well, easiest to answer of all. It wasn't raining the day we saw the house.

We were the poster children for why it's worth hiring a home inspector. They're experts at telling the unvarnished, painful truth. They identify the smells, see the leak streaks, carry flashlights, and take great professional pride in pulverizing potential, demolishing dreams, and highlighting harsh realities behind façades of charm. We pay them to shatter our romantic notions about fixer-uppers. They calmly and mercilessly put a price tag on the hyperbole of vain hope in statements like:

- "A little paint and wallpaper and this place will be perfect!"
- "What can be so hard about spackling?"
- "I'll bet there's hardwood under this shag carpeting."

Here are the same statements translated into building inspector talk:

- "Frankly, Mr. Wilson, these old horsehair plaster-and-lath walls are crumbling so badly that they will have to be removed and replaced with drywall. That'll cost you a couple of hundred per room if you do it yourself."
- "Spackling? Forget it! Touch these walls with a putty blade and whole sections will come down. Yes, I said horsehair, the real stuff, recycled. That's some fine old-school plaster. Horsehair's the only thing holding most of it together. Of course, you'll have to put up with the inside of the house looking like ash

settling after a volcanic eruption. That and the unspeakable horrors you will undoubtedly discover hidden in the walls. Oh, and did I mention that grit will get everywhere? Yes, *everywhere*. Then the mudding and taping of the drywall will require more patience than I can clearly see you have, Mr. Wilson, so the price for hiring that step done will be considerably higher. After which you and your wife are certainly welcome to try to beat the odds by painting and wallpapering together!"

- "You'll be happy to know that you guessed right, Mr. Wilson. Hardwood does lurk under the shag. It's been badly damaged in a number of places. Lookie here, see how my screwdriver blade goes through this wood like it was Styrofoam? Well, it ain't hardwood no more. By the way, now that the heavy smell of cooking has faded, have you noticed that other odor? Whatever you decide to do about the hardwood floors, this shag carpeting has got to go. The former tenants clearly had untrained cats and children who marked their territory. Need I say more?"

Building inspectors are a great idea, but they weren't around when we bought this house. Enamored with the vision of what we thought the house would look like with a little effort, we were deer in the headlights of the eighteen-wheeler Realtor who sold us the place.

During the extended period of living with three kids in what quickly became our radical renovation site, we took a night out and went to see a movie. It was called *The Money Pit*. We laughed until tears ran down our cheeks . . . neither of us willing to admit that we were actually crying. With minor alterations, we were trying to fix a cash crevasse. In an uncanny way, the nightmare in which we were living had taken on such gigantic proportions that it became comic. I wasn't sure I believed in

Murphy's Law until I lived in Murphy's house. Good friends waded into our gritty world and helped us. Sometimes they laughed at us, but mostly they laughed with us.

♥   Two can live cheaper than one, especially if one
♥   of them is a gerbil.
♥   —unknown

Here's a poignant example. Sherrie and I had a commitment one evening and arranged for a high school girl to watch our kids. An event occurred that night that we had to piece together from fractured testimony after the fact. This girl, whom we will call Liz, was a responsible young lady, anxious to do a good job and secure further employment. Knowing our three kids were young, she hoped for years of supervisory work. Apparently the night went without particular cause for alarm until after the children were safely in bed. She stepped into the bathroom for a moment. When she flushed the toilet, the contents detoured from their assigned route and poured through the ceiling in our dining room downstairs.

When we returned that night, nothing seemed amiss. But after I took the sitter home, I heard the distinct sound of a drip as I passed through the dining room on my way to the kitchen. One of the benefits of owning an old house is a set of finely tuned senses, alert to the frequent sights, sounds, and smells of something not right (senses you wish you had possessed *before* the purchase). I stepped back into the dining room and flipped the light switch. One corner of the ceiling looked as if someone had tried to fashion a plaster basketball net. The horsehair was gamely doing its job of keeping the plaster up. But it was no match for the torrent that had descended from above. The dining room floor was awash. I dashed to the kitchen to retrieve my well-worn flashlight and approached the strange eruption site. The light revealed a large, dark section of cast iron drainpipe that looked intact from where I was standing. But even I could tell it had something to do with the disaster in which I was wading.

The plumber patiently explained to me that the settling of the house had changed the angle of the drainpipe to the point where water had promoted corrosion. He stood on the ladder and said, "Lookie here, see how my screwdriver blade goes through this cast iron like it was Styrofoam? It ain't cast iron no more." Unfortunately, the pipe, like the floor on which I was standing, had been installed in the house before Styrofoam was invented!

Twenty years have come and gone. Those six years of housework were much more about homework. Our marriage survived (and thrived) through the tears and laughter of those experiences. That old house and all its problems belong to someone else now. We warned them. But they had a glazed look in their eyes. I heard the wife murmur something about paint and wallpaper . . .

LAUGH LESSON

At some point in your marriage—whether you rent, pay a mortgage, or own—you will be faced with a certain level of home repairs. Maybe one of you truly is Mr. or Ms. Fix-It, or maybe neither of you knows one end of a screwdriver from the other. When those home repair surprises happen, you can nag each other about what *should* have been done previously or what *needs* to be done now. Or you can calmly de-cide the best course of action, take a breath, think about what could have been worse, and then laugh. You'll need a little mirth and levity when the bill arrives!

Neil is a part-time pastor and full-time writer, editor, and project manager for The Livingstone Corporation, with offices in Illinois (but he lives in Wisconsin—go figure). Two of his three kids live with their families in old houses. That's how Neil still gets his yearly dose of horsehair plaster dust, cast iron shards, and dry-wall mud. For more on Livingstone, go to ***www.LivingstoneCorp.com***.

21

Jesus Laughed

Jeff Allen

The first recorded party that Jesus attended was a wedding. And He made sure everybody had a great time. We need to remember that God invented marriage, and He shows up with unexpected ways to make them work— and answers our prayers.

C. S. Lewis once posed the question (and I am paraphrasing mainly because I am too lazy to look up the actual quote) how different Christianity might have been if the Gospel writers had penned, ". . . and Jesus laughed." I only mention it because my wife, Tami, and I have come to the conclusion that by the way our Savior answers our prayers, He must have a great sense of humor.

For example, when we decided to have children years ago, we prayed for patience, tolerance, love, and understanding. These, we felt, were virtues that would only come to us with some kind of divine revelation. It would have been nice if God had just sprinkled some kind of fairy dust through our heating vents and we had woken up more patient, kind, loving, and understanding. What actually happened was this. In His loving way, He gave us not one but *two* ADHD children. Those of you who have hyperactive children know that there is no better way to learn those virtues than raising ADHD boys and girls.

Of course, I myself was hyperactive. But in my day, "the Dinosaur Days" as my offspring would say, doctors didn't have a name for hyperactivity. If I was anything, I was OLT: Obnoxious Little Twit.

Some teachers would drag me out into the hall and slam me against the lockers. I actually had one teacher head-butt me; that's right, head-butt me. I wonder if *she* prayed for patience, tolerance, love, and understanding.

So imagine my surprise when the school called years later and said to me, "I believe your son is hyperactive."

"What's that?" I asked, somewhat perplexed.

They went on to explain it, and I yelled back to my wife, "Honey, there's a name for it!"

Honestly, does this announcement come as news to *any* parent? Did any of your jaws drop when the school called and told *you*? The first day my wife and I dropped our son off at kindergarten, it was all we could do to keep from laughing. Some perky woman looked at us and gushed, "We will have so much fun!"

To which my wife and I mumbled, "We're sure you will." Then we proceeded right to Wal-Mart and purchased our first answering machine. Call it prophecy, but I felt I would be screening calls between 8:00 AM and 3:00 PM the rest of my natural life.

The principal called me at home less than a week later to inform me that my boy would not sit in his chair and was disrupting the entire class. He then went on to ask me for advice on what to do.

"Open the back door and let him loose. That's what we do at home," I replied. "He'll come back when he's tired—he always does." I also suggested that they check his hair for ticks when he returned because he likes to crawl through the shrubbery. I don't think he took my advice. When I hung up, I prayed for *his* patience, tolerance, love, and understanding.

♥
♥   **If you have only one child, you're not officially**
♥   **a parent . . . because you always know who**
♥   **did it!**
♥
—Bill Cosby

I believe wholeheartedly in the power of prayer and in God's desire to answer our prayers. Life's lessons come through adversity. C. S. Lewis also said that suffering is God's megaphone. Those of us who raise ADHD children have heard that megaphone, and in hindsight we can see that such adversity gave us our greatest lessons as parents. Certainly it was an answer to prayer—not the answer I would have expected, but it is not my universe.

I cannot deny that because of our children and their proclivity toward chaos, my wife and I are more patient, tolerant, loving, and understanding.

Often after "one of those days," Tami and I collapse, exhausted, onto the couch, look at each other, and smile. Then we look at the heavens, and say, "All right, all right, we hear You!"

. . . and Jesus laughed.

LAUGH LESSON

The trials of raising children can draw couples together. Ultimately, we learn to see the humor in the circular aspects of life, when we who were once the children who drove our parents and others crazy suddenly find ourselves on the parent side of the equation.

Adapted from the comedy of Jeff Allen. Jeff has been entertaining audiences, and his family, for many years. To learn more about Jeff, his life, ministry, and humor, and to read his articles and blog, visit *www.JeffAllenComedy.com*.

22

Camp Trust-a-Lot

Rhonda Rhea

We all have to live in the world, but our interest in certain parts of the world can certainly bring to light some striking differences between spouses.

I am a city girl. I think I could've been born in the middle of the woods and I would still have to classify myself a city girl. I've never felt that need to "enjoy nature"—never really longed for the great outdoors. I think I do have a great sense of adventure . . . for indoor adventure. I enjoy a nice tree as much as anyone, but isn't that why God made picture windows? And for every tree, there are a zillion bugs. That pretty much ruins it for me even before we talk about the sweat factor.

My family and I have a nice home. We pay money for this nice home, and then we pay more to fill it with every convenience. Camping, as I see it, is leaving this nice home (while still paying for it) and leaving all my conveniences to go to a place that has exactly zero conveniences. Then you pay the campground for the lack of conveniences.

Does anyone else see a sad irony here? Not to mention that no matter what the weather forecast, the camping I participate in seems to always involve a generous dose of rain.

A while back, I reluctantly agreed to go camping with my family. I can't overemphasize the word *reluctantly*. You can still see the fingernail marks from my house (with all the conveniences) to the hot, bug-infested campground.

> ❤ **A man has five items in his bathroom: a tooth-**
> ❤ **brush, shaving cream, razor, a bar of soap, and a**
> ❤ **towel from the Marriott. The average number of**
> ❤ **items in a typical woman's bathroom is 337. A man**
> ❤ **would not be able to identify most of these items.**
>
> —unknown

We happened to be there on the hottest weekend of the millennium—somewhere around 147 degrees. My five children, my camping-enthusiast husband, and I squished our sweaty bodies into the three-person tent. Did I mention the 147-degree temperature? And that nylon (as in tent) retains and magnifies heat? How about the buzzard-size mosquitoes that threatened to carry off my children? Did I mention those? I fought off the urge to mumble, "Are we having fun yet?"

My husband, ever the indoor-outdoor adventurer, suggested that we sit in a sweaty family circle and tell our favorite Bible stories. When it was my turn, all I could think of was the children of Israel wandering in the wilderness. They were forced to camp in tents for forty years. It was stern *punishment* for their sinful rebellion against God. Richie and the kids were all deeply moved by my heartfelt sharing. They seemed to relish the opportunity to identify with such a significant story from the Bible.

As I lay there trying not to think about bugs, snakes, and assorted disgusting and/or frightening members of the bionetwork, I do remember clicking my heels together with a "There's no place like home." But when I opened my eyes, I was still there—up to my eyeballs in bugs and swimming in a sea of sweat.

I'm amazed how camping forces people to think Godward. Some out of awe for the beauty of nature. Some through faith-stretching experiences. Others out of fear of those bionetwork members. Whatever the case, we can trust an all-powerful Creator, knowing that He is always perfectly able to care for us and that He has a plan. He had a plan for Jonah even in the belly of the big fish. He had a plan for the children of Israel even as they wandered in the wilderness and camped in suffocating tents for forty years. I knew He had a plan for my life—even when I was whining about my own wilderness experience. And even while I was camping, I really always knew that whatever the circumstances, His arms were strong enough to keep me in the center of His plan for me.

I didn't have to seek the Lord very long the morning after our night of camping before I was delivered. Richie is a merciful man, so we left the campground early—before I had time to complain about more than fifty or sixty inconveniences. On the way home (to all our wonderful and even more deeply appreciated conveniences), I could hardly contain my joy. Revival almost broke out in the car.

LAUGH LESSON

We don't have to like (read: love) everything our spouses value highly. But the efforts we make to experience alongside them will be appreciated. Discovering what it is about those activities that they love can lead us to unexpected delights. After all, the hot showers we love feel even better after a weekend in the mud . . .

Adapted from *Amusing Grace: Hilarity and Hope in the Everyday Calamity of Motherhood* by Rhonda Rhea, Cook Communications Ministries, 2003. For all things Rhonda Rhea, check out ***www.RhondaRhea.org***.

23

Of Skunks and Men

John Pickerl

Some situations are ripe for embarrassment. In fact, John, and his wife, Cindy, found that they were very "ripe" indeed . . .

The animal had apparently been living under our front stoop for years, sleeping during the day with its tail up against the warm foundation, bothering no one, taking its Prozac, and minding its own business.

Until the landscape workers with the nuclear-powered chain saws arrived.

There we were, our happy family sitting around the breakfast table on Sunday morning, our five-year-old twin boys flinging syrupy waffle parts at each other. Cindy was exhausted from a week of this; I was exhausted from five minutes of it, and the jury was still out on our having a third child. A typical Sunday morning.

When up through the ducts there arose such a smell.

I thought of the sulfur they have down in hell.

At first it smelled like burning wires, so I was thinking electrical fire . . . no problem. I'll just apply that principle Mr. Wenz taught us in electric shop class in high school: "All right, you guys, the next one who flings syrupy waffle parts gets a detention!" But in a matter of seconds we realized that the smoky smell of a mere electrical fire probably wouldn't cause our nose hairs to spontaneously combust. *It must be something worse,* I thought.

And it was. A skunk had indeed expressed its displeasure with the workers' noise, displeasure that the furnace then sent throughout the house. And into the furniture. And into clothes buried in drawers. Into everything.

The smell then transferred to anything we touched, with no reduction in intensity, going from our clothes to my in-laws' furniture to anything set on that furniture, and so on unto the third and fourth generations. For you stereo buffs, skunk smell has the same fidelity as digital audiotape.

> ❤ **A man will pay two dollars for a one dollar item**
> ❤ **he needs. A woman will pay one dollar for a two**
> ❤ **dollar item that she doesn't need, but it's on sale.**
> ❤   —unknown

During those first few minutes that we could stand being in the house after the attack, we didn't realize that the skunk was on the *outside.* Not knowing that the workers also smelled it and fled, we assumed that any aroma potent enough to be banned under the Geneva convention must be coming from inside the house . . . like from the crawl space.

So, being the dad of the house and feeling an obligation to Do Something—or more precisely, to Do Something Stupid—I took a flashlight and went to investigate. Understand that I had no plan in mind, no trap in hand, no idea what I would do were I to actually encounter this creature. I simply went forth to waddle around our four-foot-high crawl space, dressed in my Sunday best, ready to shine a powerful beam of light into the eyes of a nocturnal creature who *detests* light. And can prove it.

To show how bad the smell was down there, I carried the flashlight in one hand and—I am not kidding—an open bottle of ammonia in the other. This solvent, which burns your eyes and lungs, actually provides relief from the hellish sulfur of skunk spray. At least it did for me, down in the crawl space. My foray into the crawl space achieved nothing, so abandoning the search, we drove to church (Our Lady of the Expensive Building Campaign) in what is, for our family, a typical Sunday morning ready-for-worship frame of mind.

CINDY *(sniffing her clothes)*: Do we smell? I think we smell.

ME *(sniffing my clothes)*: Nah. It's just our singed nose hairs.

CINDY: No, honey. I think that stuff got on us.

FIVE-YEAR-OLD SON: I forgot my triceratops.

OTHER FIVE-YEAR-OLD SON: Can I have a cookie?

ME: You'll have toys and treats in Sunday school. Anyway, honey, that stuff couldn't have gotten on us, could it?

CINDY: I think it did.

FIVE-YEAR-OLD SON: I need my triceratops!

OTHER FIVE-YEAR-OLD SON: I don't *want* treats in Sunday school!

ME *(pulling into church parking lot)*: Don't whine! You really think so, honey?

FIVE-YEAR-OLD SON: I need my triceratops! Waaahhh!

OTHER FIVE-YEAR-OLD SON: I don't *want* treats in Sunday school! Waaahhh!

ME *(parking the car)*: Stop it right now, you two! NOW!

TWO FIVE-YEAR-OLD SON *(being half-dragged into church, hands protecting their bottoms)*: Waaahhh!

US *(trying unsuccessfully to swat their bottoms)*: I said STOP IT!! We're at church!

EVERY OTHER PARENT WITHIN EARSHOT *(thinking)*: I'm glad *my* children don't behave like that.

Actually on this particular day, due to the interruption of my trip into the crawl space, we were late. So late that the service had already begun. So late that we needed to sit in the front.

I now know how the Pope feels as he walks down the aisle of a church full of people, adorned in full regalia, and everyone turns to notice. Except we were adorned with something far less subtle than even the Pope's robes. As we passed each row on our way to the only available seats, ardent worshipers pointed and gasped as if to say, "Is it really them?" Many were so overcome with reverence that their eyes rolled back and their knees buckled (and we're not even charismatic!). One person who had a cold so severe he couldn't have smelled his own mustache on fire sniffed and said, "Did somebody get sprayed by a skunk?"

But it was the pastor who best captured the mood of the congregation with a quote from Matthew 24: "There will be weeping and gnashing of teeth."

We moved out of the house; the skunk surrendered to agents from the Bureau of Alcohol, Tobacco, and Pest Control; and we had the house fumigated by sweaty workers who don't practice what they bleach . . .

By the following December I was able to put enough extra money aside to buy Cindy a nice Christmas present. Something she always wanted. Something every woman wants: a new sewer line to replace the old one that had collapsed just in time for the holidays, causing sewer water to back up into the basement with a stench that drove us to our knees in a desperate plea to God for something—anything—to mask the awful smell. Something like maybe a deranged skunk carrying an open bottle of ammonia.

LAUGH LESSON

Embarrassing situations can cause us to fume, to turn on each other, or to hibernate (of course, if you smell like a skunk, maybe the third option wouldn't be such a bad idea). In any case, rare yet wise are those who can laugh at themselves, even when everyone else has already started!

John is a husband, father, homeowner, employee of Wheaton College, and former animal lover. You can contact him via e-mail at *pickstick32@att.net*.

24

The Great Experiment

Rhonda Rhea

Rhonda and her husband, Richie, continue their great experiment, spending a lifetime discovering over and over how marriage is the merging of two very different individuals.

Marriage is definitely a step of faith. I think it's probably The Great Experiment. It's hard not to feel that preparing for marriage is like standing next to the edge of a cliff. "Will he be as sweet one month after the marriage as he was one month before?" "Will she use my razor?" "Will he roll the toothpaste from the bottom or turn out to be one of those dreaded 'middle-squeezers'?" "Can she learn to cook like my mother?" "Can he be reprogrammed in correct toilet-seat repositioning?" So many unknowns. Such a step of faith.

After over twenty years of marriage, I'm pretty sure Richie and I are past the probationary period. Ours happens to be a marriage experiment gone very *right*. Twenty-plus years and we still like each other. We're going for a record.

I'm sorry to say that I have seen some of those "Frankenstein" kinds of marriage experiments. Have you ever seen one of those situations where Mr. Nitro marries Ms. Glycerin? Seems everyone near them ends up with smoking hair and no eyebrows. Take cover! Explosive marriage incoming! I'd sooner camp out in the lab of a vision-impaired nuclear physicist.

Genesis 2:23–24 tells us about the first mysterious marriage experiment.

> The man said,
>> "This is now bone of my bones
>> and flesh of my flesh;
>> she shall be called 'woman,'
>>> for she was taken out of man."
> For this reason a man will leave his father and mother and
> be united to his wife, and they will become one flesh.

Now that's one *out there* kind of experiment. The example seems to suggest taking two individuals from different families, different backgrounds—even different genders—and making them one. Intriguing hypothesis. Could that really work?

In the course of our marriage experiment, like any experiment, things haven't always turned out as expected. The experiment has included experiences that have revealed in their own quirky way that although God's plan for marriage may be perfect, those of us working that plan are far from perfect. What follows illustrates the truth that love is a many-slimed thing.

When I was a kid, the cure-all was Vicks VapoRub. If you couldn't slime away your ailment, it probably wasn't curable. I was greased down so many times growing up I thought my parents had me confused with their 1968 Chevy. I'm almost sure they thought that with a vapo-lube I'd be good as new. At least they never tried to change my oil. Still, I can't imagine why, but there's something awfully comforting about sliding into bed (and I do mean sliding) with slime oozing out of your jammies. I don't know how I could've felt more protected from the symptoms of the ailment du jour. Maybe that explains my affection for various body creams today—all the same comfort with less of the vapo odors.

My husband is convinced that lotion is scented slime imported from the place of the dead. I have no doubt he would sooner wallow in lard than use one of my creams. As a matter of fact, he says he can't under-stand how anyone can put that stuff on a clean body without feeling all dirty again.

He even goes so far as to make one of those pained-looking faces after I've driven his car, post-lotion. He says it makes his steering wheel gooey. Picture him trying to drive using only a thumb and forefinger from each hand. Such a commotion over a little lotion!

Me? I love the stuff. It's sort of medicinal and therapeutic all at the same time. I guess I'm a lotion lover because I'm one of those rather dry women (skin, not wit). If you're like me and can make sparks by rub-bing your hands together, you know what I mean.

I consider myself creamed to perfection when I'm so greasy that my fingers keep sliding right off my computer keyboard. If you're ever read-ing something I've written and you get to "dk7n>le#i4ig*20;slhc&mo$b," you don't need to worry. It's most likely a little lotion slip and you can picture me smiling.

If I were Balm Queen, no one would ever be lotion-poor. Lotion for all! After I made sure no one was deprived of his or her lotion, I would go out and swim in my own personal pool of lotion. Of course, I'd never be able to get out. Just try climbing up a pool ladder when you've been swimming in lotion. That's okay. I'd be satisfied to soak in my lotion ocean.

> **I'm certainly glad my husband [Billy] and I are not exactly alike; if that were the case, one of us wouldn't be necessary.**
>
> —Ruth Graham

Just as lotion satisfies a dry woman, a thirsty soul can be satisfied by seeking the God who hydrates us at the very center of who we are. Psalm 63:1–3 (HCSB) says:

> God, You are my God; I eagerly seek You. I thirst for You; my body faints for You in a land that is dry, desolate, and without water.
>
> So I gaze on You in the sanctuary to see Your strength and Your glory.
>
> My lips will glorify You because Your faithful love is better than life.

He is the God who quenches. When we seek Him and desire Him in this dry place, He satisfies oh so much more than the best lotions and creams. He fills our every real need by His strength and for His glory. And it's all out of His faithful love for us. Better than lotion. Better than life!

I love sharing the message of the satisfied life with others. I love passing it on to my children. They're receiving the message better than they are my lotion notions. I thought they would love it, for instance, when I bought the tissues with lotion added right in. I asked one of my sons how he liked them. He said to direct all other such questions to his attorney. There's a lot of his father in that boy.

LAUGH LESSON

Seeing the big picture of God's design for marriage keeps things in their proper place. All the positive discoveries made through the marital process are part of the Designer's plan. And His plan often includes laughter.

Adapted from *Who Put the Cat in the Fridge? Serving Up Hope and Hilarity Family Style* by Rhonda Rhea, Cook Communications Ministries, 2005. For all things Rhonda Rhea, check out ***www.RhondaRhea.org***.

25

Extended Family

John Branyan

A wedding often turns out to be the first of a great many family events to follow. The crossover experience can create a lot of memorable and humorous moments.

Probably the most difficult times in a relationship are the holidays. That seems to be when the relationship is most strained. Because there's nothing like a big celebration to bring out rage in the loved ones.

Lori's favorite time of year is Christmas. She can hardly contain herself in anticipation. Every year, at the beginning of October, she starts in, "What are we going to do about the tree?" I know what tree she's talking about—the Christmas tree! I shrug and say, "Honey—it's October! It's been up this long . . ."

The first year we were married, prior to Christmas, the men in the family pulled me aside to review my upcoming responsibilities. "John, it's the man's job to establish holiday traditions! It's your awesome responsibility to set down family traditions that will be observed for generations to come. Now go forth and make us proud!"

So, with that in mind, we hunted down and hand-cut our first family Christmas tree, a time-honored tradition that we have since quit. Because it's a hassle. It's too hard to find the perfect tree out there that everyone will agree is the symbol of yuletide festivities. The first year we did it, I lucked out. We found a great tree, two houses down, right in the front yard . . . and it already had lights on it too.

♥ **Any married man should forget his mistakes.**

♥ **There's no use in two people remembering the**

♥ **same thing.**

♥

—unknown

The thing is, Christmas is not just a time for the immediate family to get together for tradition's sake. No, no, extended loved ones have to show up from all the sectors of the galaxy. All gathered together at one place, at one time, for one purpose—friction.

Now, believe me, a family reunion doesn't have to be a bad experience. Just follow my very simple rule: Don't go to *your* family reunion. But sometimes you can't help it, like when you're married. When you are married, you have to go to the in-laws' reunion, because if you don't show up, they will think you don't like them. And you don't want them to know that for sure. Sometimes it's just unavoidable. You eventually figure out that when you said, "I do," the small print explained that one of the ways to finish that statement is, "I do go to your family reunions."

This year, Lori's family reunion was at her uncle's place. Uncle Jack owns a little cottage right down on the lake. That's where the family gathered. As everyone was arriving, Jack was down on the pier, standing by his new boat, insisting that we all come and look at it. A brand-new speedboat that we had to see because it was a beauty.

I heard him as soon as I climbed out of the car. "Ol' Jack got hisself a new speedboat this year and she's a beauty! Beauty! I'm sure you ain't seen a boat quite like this, and she's a beauty! *Bass Tracker* magazine wrote about this boat and you know what *Bass Tracker* magazine said? 'Beauty! A beauty of a boat!' If I was to use one word to describe this boat, I would have to use the word . . . *beauty!* B . . . U . . . T . . . Y! Beauty. Hey, John, come here and take a look at this boat. What do you think of her?"

"That's a beauty, Uncle Jack."

"You bet she is, boy. She will do six . . . hundred . . . miles an hour! Hop in. I'm going to teach you how to ski."

So I jumped into the boat next to Jack, and all my brothers-in-law came running. "Hey, come on down to the boat. Jack's going to teach John how to ski. It'll be fun to watch! He'll probably die!" I won't go into the painful, humiliating, and absolutely terrifying half hour that followed except to note some of my brilliant discoveries. First, don't try to learn to ski with a lunatic at the controls of the boat. Second, the one-size-fits-all skis should also be labeled, "except John." And third, while learning to let go of the ski rope once one has fallen, I also found out that the human nose will hold two and a half gallons of water!

LAUGH LESSON

Extended family members bring both stresses and delights into life. You can easily focus on the irritants rather than the humor. It boils down to how you're willing to look at life. If you ignore humor, all you're left with is irritation. But if you are determined to include humor in your life, even the irritants can become gateways into hilarity.

Adapted from DVD presentation *Wedlocked* by John Branyan. John has humorous takes on much more than marriage. You can find out more about John at ***www.JohnBranyan.com***.

26

We Came, We Bought, We Suffered

John Pickerl

The decision to buy a house is a greater commitment than most couples realize, and it often looms large over the history of a marriage.

My earliest memory in life is the day we bought our house. Most people can trace their memories back to age three or so, and I used to be able to. But no more. I remember everything after the closing, but have no recollection of any part of my life before we became homeowners.

This is because of a basic design flaw in the human memory: It doesn't kick in until the onset of stress. And before we bought a house, life was comparatively stress free. Nothing tests a marriage (or a person's sanity) more than this first *major* purchase.

Just as normal people (that is, renters) have no memory of the womb—when life was carefree and all you did was float serenely, suspended in liquid who-knows-what, sleeping whenever you wanted, having loving relatives read nursery rhymes to you through your mother's stomach—so also I, as a homeowner, have no memory of life as a renter, when the responsibility to fix stuff was somebody else's.

After we bought our house, and I'd try to sleep, floating serenely on my bed, I could hear the sound of loving building contractors reading estimates to me through the walls:

Jack and Bill
Most gladly will
Go up to fix your rafters.
They'll come down,
You'll wear a frown,
Making payments ever after.

On our first morning in the house following the closing—or The Morning After, as we now think of it—I was taking a shower, feeling on top of the world, thrilled to be a homeowner, singing Crosby, Stills, and Nash's "Our house is a very very very fine house," oblivious to the problems of the world, oblivious to the amount of debt I was in, oblivious to the corroded bathtub, oblivious to the corroded plumbing under the tub, oblivious to my wife in the laundry room directly below. Life was good. I had stepped into the American Dream. I was in love, in marriage, and in a home of my own!

And now it was time for the alarm to go off.

"Honey," she called, with the soothing voice of a nightingale, "is water supposed to be falling down from the bathtub onto the washing machine?"

Now I don't know about you, but when I hear the words *water* and *fall*, the image that comes to mind is not "bathtub" and "washing machine." I picture a place in Hawaii, where a sheet of blue liquid satin cascades off a rock formation into a pool below and caresses the tan skin of beautiful Polynesian maidens who exist only in travel brochures. I don't picture a torrent of soapsuds and hair globs splattering down onto the only appliance in the house manufactured after World War II.

Dripping wet, wrapped in a towel, I did the manly husband thing, traipsing downstairs to the laundry room to analyze the problem, using a jerky birdlike motion of the head to look alternately up and down, first up at the bathtub drain above and then down at the washing machine below. Up. Down. Up. Down. Bathtub drain. Washing machine. Bathtub drain. Washing machine. Then there flashed in my brain that one teensy-weensy detail I had overlooked before we bought our house: the whole-house inspection.

> ♥ This country is great. It's the only place where
> ♥ you can borrow money for a down payment, get
> ♥ a first and second mortgage, and call yourself a
> ♥ homeowner.
>
> —unknown

Cindy and I have learned a valuable lesson that I would now like to pass on to renters everywhere in case you should ever get the urge to buy a house, an urge that people seem to develop at a certain stage in life (like after they've gone in for a root canal, but the dentist slips on a banana peel and gives them a lobotomy instead): Never, under any circumstances, buy a house without first ordering a professional whole-house inspection. In fact, never buy *anything* without a whole-house inspection. Don't buy a pair of *shoes* without a whole-house inspection:

YOU: Excuse me, do you have these in a size nine?

SALESMAN: We sure do. Will that be cash or charge today?

YOU: Not so fast! You think I'm gullible or something? I'm not buy-ing *anything* without a whole-house inspection. Where's your house?

The plumbing under the tub was indeed corroded. I was able to determine that by comparing it to the plumbing in the rest of the house, which was also corroded.

Fortunately, while in graduate school I worked as a plumber's assis-tant, during which time I learned enough about the trade to say with confidence that if I had to make a living at it, I'd starve. I know enough about plumbing to dial the phone number of a real plumber—but only *after* going to the plumbing supply place and "investing" in expensive torches and pipe cutters and numerous fittings, all the wrong size, and attempting to do it myself. Then and only then do I call our regular plumber, John DePue, who in exchange for this promotional an-nouncement, can now afford to stay at the luxurious Sands Hotel, in beautiful downtown Las Vegas.

John always seems to enjoy working at our house, possibly because of the extra time he gets to rack up, first by pointing at my attempt and laughing uproariously before finally composing himself long enough to undo the damage—precious minutes that add up like dog years on a plumber's bill.

Over time, our morning-after discovery about the plumbing was reenacted in other areas about which I know nothing, such as roofing. One blustery day we were out on the patio when pieces of fiberglass in-sulation began to swirl down on us. I had checked the weather forecast the night before, and it said nothing about a chance of insulation, so I was pretty sure an umbrella was not the tool du jour.

From up on the roof, the view was spectacular. I could look down onto our neighbor's yard. I could look down onto our patio. I could look down onto our bedroom through the hole left by the shingles and insulation that had blown away.

It turned out we had *dry rot*, a term really meaning "wet rot," which is the process whereby leaking rainwater over time reduces sturdy lumber to the density of driftwood. We also had windows that wouldn't open, doors that wouldn't close, and old cedar siding that was dark green with gold trim. Cindy couldn't stand it (although, Notre Dame fans loved it).

And so we hired a contractor, who happened to be a friend of the family. (Helpful tip: *Never* hire a contractor who is a friend of the family. In the end, you develop hatred for each other. Instead, hire someone whom you *already* hate. It's just one less thing you'll have to do later.) He walked me through the house with a clipboard and a tape measure, stopping every so often to measure the square footage of money I would pay him over the next five months.

"So what all do we need?" I said.

"Oh, nothing major," he said. "Just tear off the roof, extend the roof line, replace the sheeting and shingles, get all new siding and gutters and windows and doors—"

"Whew, that's a relief," I said. "I was afraid you were going to say, 'Tuck-point the chimney, gut the bathroom, replace all the plumbing, and rebuild the bathroom.'"

"—and tuck-point the chimney, gut the bathroom, replace all the plumbing, and rebuild the bathroom."

And so it went: refinancing our mortgage; tearing the roof completely off during the rainiest February this side of Borneo; having rain get behind the new wallpaper in the kitchen that we had just redecorated the year before; running out of money; borrowing more; asking the contractor not to cut corners; being cursed at by the contractor; reminding the contractor who was employing whom; dodging birds that came down the chimney and out through the furnace; having shingle cinders and drywall dust get everywhere, including the toothpaste; and being without a bathroom—all these things converged to where I became such a raving lunatic that Cindy and the boys were ready to go anywhere for some peace and quiet. Like a Guns N' Roses concert.

LAUGH LESSON

One of the greatest reminders that we live in a fallen world comes to us through home ownership. It is a reminder that keeps on reminding, year after year. No matter how diligent one is about maintenance, things still surprisingly and inconveniently break, leak, fail, and completely collapse. Welcome to the dream that can so easily become a comedy!

John lives in Illinois and keeps everyone around him in good humor, even Cindy. You can contact John via e-mail at *pickstick32@att.net*.

27

Ideals, Expectations, and Reality

Jim Smith

Marriage is a continual reality check. Expectations and ideals pass through the grinder of reality, and they get sifted into something different. Sometimes they get better.

While conducting a marriage-enrichment seminar, I noticed that one particular woman was taking copious notes throughout my entire presentation. Of course, I was flattered. A speaker always feels complimented when somebody feels that what he or she is saying is worth writing down. This lady just kept writing.

At the end of the seminar, however, I discovered that she had been doing some creative writing. In her notes, she had given a curious slant to what I had been saying that weekend.

She had made two columns on her paper. At the top of the first column was written, "What Every Man Expects When He Gets Married." Across from that she had written, "What He Gets." On the second page she had done the same thing from the woman's perspective.

Under "What Every Man Expects," she had written, "The ideal wife." I had mentioned that a lot of men today seem to want a combination of Halle Berry, Jennifer Aniston, Mother Teresa, Kristi Yamaguchi, and Meg Whitman. Unfortunately, women like that don't exist. Every woman wants a man with the qualities of Patrick Dempsey, Mario Lopez, Billy Graham, LeBron James, and Bill Gates all rolled into one. Obviously, we all have to make some significant trade-offs!

So my listener wrote that a man expects a wife who . . .

- is always beautiful and cheerful.
- could have married a movie star but wants only you.
- has hair that never needs curlers or a beauty shop.
- has beauty that won't run in a rainstorm, because she doesn't wear makeup. Her glow is natural.
- is never sick; she's just allergic to jewelry and Italian leather shoes.
- insists that moving the furniture by herself is good for her figure.
- is an expert at cooking, cleaning house, and fixing the car or computer.
- is an expert at painting the house. She even hangs wallpaper by herself.
- has favorite hobbies of mowing the lawn and shoveling snow.
- hates credit cards, and her favorite expression is "What can I do for you, dear?"
- thinks you have Einstein's brain and look like Mr. America.
- says she loves you because you're so sexy.

Then across from that, she had written that what he gets is a woman who . . .

- speaks 140 words a minute with gusts up to 180.
- was once a model . . . for a totem pole.

- is known as a light eater: as soon as it gets light, she starts eating.
- treats you like a god . . . offering three burnt offerings a day. Where there is smoke, there she is, cooking.
- has hair that, despite what she does, looks like an explosion in a steel wool factory.
- uses a broom only to fly somewhere.
- can find you if you get lost—just open your wallet.
- fights with the neighbors just to keep in practice until you get home.
- lets you know you have only two faults: everything you say and everything you do.

During the seminar, I had commented about the irony between the first days and the last days of a troubled marriage. I had said, "It's fun to go to weddings, isn't it? I go to quite a few; I perform quite a few, in fact. Sometimes I think of those starry-eyed couples, so in love, so infatuated with each other. Sometimes you just have to wonder, how can anything that starts out so wonderful end so tragically?"

On page two of her notes, my listener was a little more poetic. Under "What Every Woman Expects," she had written:

The Ideal Husband

One well groomed and charming, a dashing one, too,
could have married great women but desires only you.
No five o'clock shadow ever crosses his face.
He's always dressed in the latest, each hair in its place.
He's never sick, a tower of strength all for you.
He's allergic to golf clubs . . . and snowmobiles, too.

He insists you not strain yourself in any way.
He hangs up his clothes and does the dishes each day.
He's an expert in making and managing money,
and he's generous when giving costly gifts to his honey.
He rules his well-behaved children with hand firm and fair.
He's a painter, a plumber, an expert at lawn care.
He's a great conversationalist, well versed in all things.
He's a right cheerful fellow; he whistles and sings.
He's always asking, "What would you like to do?"
He loves you so much, just because you are you!

Then, across from that, under "What She Gets," my listener had written, still in verse:

He grunts: once if by land, two if by sea,
while glued to his chair by the color TV.
His hair, what's left, needs a brush and shampoo.
And his chest? Well, it sunk, irretrievably, too.
He snaps at the children and kicks the poor dog.
After wolfing his supper, he sleeps like a log.
He expects T-bone steak as his bill of fare,
but the budget allows only filet of mare.
The paint is all chipped, and the front porch is sagging.
You mention it once and get scolded for nagging.
He needs one night a week to go out with the boys.
He thinks speedboats and cycles are his well-deserved toys.
When you'd like to find out if he loves you or no,
he just shrugs and says, "I'm still here, aren't I? So?"

At the bottom of the page she had written:

How amazing to me is God's wonderful plan.
He takes imperfect woman and imperfect man,
two quite different persons, and when He's done,
they're molded and formed by His hands into one.
A wedding is just the foundation block,
but marriage goes on building rock upon rock
until you're melded together through trial and test,
for God makes good things better, and better things best.

That's what Mary Pelto was writing while I was speaking. Thanks, Mary, for letting me share your creativity with others.

LAUGH LESSON

Every marriage involves six people: the two people each expects the other to be; the two people as they see themselves, and the two people as they truly are. These six people relate throughout marriage, and the results, though sometimes tragic, can also be hilarious. A golden lesson to remember is that you are not nearly as great a catch as you tend to think you are. A little smiling humility goes a long way in the rough-and-tumble of life.

Adapted from *Learning to Live with the One You Love*. The late Jim ("Jimbo") Smith was a veteran of Youth for Christ and a much-loved staff member of Highland Park Presbyterian Church in Dallas, Texas.

28

The Twenty-One Year Mile Marker

John Branyan

Life will include both sweetness and saltiness. Healthy people learn how to cry as well as how to laugh. Ultimately, reaching the end of life, like reaching the end of a book, ought to result in a combination of deep satisfaction, a smile, and perhaps a tear.

Things haven't turned out in marriage quite as I expected. I thought after twenty-one years, I would have all the answers, I'd have this marriage thing figured out. I thought I'd just know what to do, and I don't. I'm still confused about the function of each gender within the relationship. You know, men and women—well women, mostly. Women are supposed to be the weaker sex. That is how they are advertised. That means I'm supposed to be the stronger sex—a role I have absolutely no idea how to fake.

Over the years, out of desperation, I have come up with the complex algebraic formula that I'm always running in my head to prove manliness. Here it is: The more dirt I can get on me, the more manly I seem. That's it. Basically, I just look for excuses to get dirty. "Lori, if you need me, I'll be out in the front yard today—landscaping. Old man of the house is going to take pick and shovel in hand and dig a huge hole right next to the mailbox. Why? Because we don't have a hole next to the mailbox. There's going to be dirt in the air, dirt in my hair, dirt under my fingernails—don't you worry about me, little lady, 'cause we men love dirt!" Just don't ask me to get the tip of my finger in the contents of a dirty diaper . . . all pretense of manliness will be out the window! The same is true about my aversion to those long, green, slimy things that tend to hang from the noses of two-year-olds. I run; Lori removes them with her bare hands! She is not the weaker sex!

Or take discipline. Women are the frontline disciplinarians at home. "You wait until your dad gets home" usually provokes a child's response, "Why?" To which the answer is, "So we can all stand around and hear him say, 'Hmmm. I don't know. What did your mother say?' "

Twenty-one years into marriage is a long way but clearly not far enough! In the midst of it all—unanswered questions, low self-esteem, confusion of roles, kids flying around the house—in the midst of all this, I'm still expected to be . . . romantic. I'm still expected to breathe fresh wind on the embers of romance. Out of nowhere she will say, "Take me someplace. Take me someplace . . . nice."

"All right. Where do you want to go?"

"I don't want to tell you where to take me. That would ruin everything. You have to think of someplace to go."

So, I get tickets to the tractor pull. That, as it turns out, is wrong.

We have many friends whose cummerbunds matched the flowers and the dresses, and who marched down the aisle and took a solemn vow, "Till death do us part." And then they parted . . . but they weren't dead.

It takes a lifetime to even learn how to love another person. To figure out what brings him or her deep, sincere joy. To learn what really annoys your spouse—so you can do it again and again. If you stick with it long enough, you'll zero in on the source of conflict. You'll figure out what causes the two of you to fight. Lori and I did. It's me.

 Marriage is an investment which pays dividends if you pay interest.

—Bob Monkhouse

I remember the first fight that I caused. It was right after we got married. I wanted to go out with the guys. Just me and the guys, like the old times. But she wanted me to stay there with her . . . and cut the cake, throw the garter, leave on time for the honeymoon. Even now, she'll sometimes get me backed into a corner, outmaneuvered, and she'll say, "John, listen, sweetie. I was just reading in *Cosmo* . . ."

Cosmo? I know I'm in trouble. Well, bring it on.

She continues, unfazed, "Here's the question they pose: If you could start all over again and wipe the slate clean—hey, look at me; this is important—if you would wipe the slate clean and start afresh, would you get married again?"

The *speed* with which you answer that question is just as crucial as the answer itself! And the truth is, after twenty-one years, the answer to that question is, "Yes!" I would marry the exact same girl again. Because what I have learned over these years is that the two of us together are somehow way better than the sum of the individual parts. She is so many things I could never be. And I'm so many things that she doesn't want to be. It's complementary. We haven't mastered it; we're still learning. I'm learning that she's like a flower—a flower with an infinite number of petals. And each petal is a little more complex and lovely than the petal that preceded it. And it's going to take a lifetime to examine every subtle nuance, every tiny little facet of her personality that makes her unique and special and different from all the rest—beautiful. And she's learning that every guy is exactly the same, as in "You might as well stick with me, baby, 'cause that's all there is."

I know her better than anyone else on the planet. She's my other half. I know her favorite color. I know how she looks in the morning. I know her shoe size. I know how she cooks (don't ever knock the microwave oven). I've discovered that she does something magical with microwave popcorn that allows her to claim it's an old family recipe. I know how she drives . . . I've got the slicked-back hair to prove it. Her motto is "Well, we pay for insurance. We might as well use it!" She does stuff with insurance I could never do. She once hit a deer that was already dead. Tore the running board off the car, knocked the wheels out of alignment—she was so upset! "Sorry, John, I didn't hit him on purpose!"

I didn't get mad. I couldn't get mad. 'Cause you know those deer-crossing signs on the road? Have you noticed they always show the deer leaping high, never laid out on the road?

And late at night, on long car trips, she'll sit up front with me when I'm driving. And she'll say, "John, this is a long trip and it's late at night, and I'm sure you're tired because it's a long trip . . . So, I'll just sit up here and keep you company, help you stay awake. " A few moments go by and she turns in the soft light of the dashboard and asks, "What are you thinking?" Before I can come up with some kind of a plausible answer out of the empty space called my brain, I notice that she's sound asleep. She's gone. So, the next chance I get, I pull into a rest area where all the other travelers gather, and I drive slowly in among all the semis idling with their lights on. I pull up nose to nose with one of the trucks, throw the car into neutral, gun the engine, and go, "Aaagghh!"

But you know what happened when all the cake had been eaten and the wedding flowers wilted, and all the thank-yous had been sent? After that, after the wedding? Then real life settled in. There's no getting around it, day-to-day life is hard. And it's mundane. And it doesn't feel the way it does when you're planning a big wedding. It doesn't feel the way it feels when you're dating. Some days it doesn't even feel like it's worth it. And every time those feelings come, I have these memories of my great-grandparents . . . Frank and Mamie. When we were little, we would go over to their house, my little brother and I, and my great-grandfather Frank would sit in his overstuffed chair by the window. And he would lean forward in that chair and talk with his hands and tell us all the stuff that little boys are supposed to know. He taught us how to bait a hook and cast a line. He taught us how to build a tree house up in the branches so the floor wouldn't sag and the roof wouldn't leak. He taught us how to sit on the handlebars of our bikes and ride them backward down the hill . . . with groceries . . .

And all afternoon in the rocking chair next to him was my great-grandmother, Mamie. She had her hands in her lap, and she rocked back and forth and looked over at him while he talked. She would occasionally shake her head and roll her eyes. And she would still laugh at the same jokes she had heard him tell a billion times before. In the middle of his stories, he would glance at her and pat her on the knee, give her a wink without ever missing a beat in the story.

As the years went by, we noticed that Mamie started having trouble remembering things . . . like recipes that used to come from her heart. Then she forgot the names of the neighbors. So my great-grandfather's job became just to be with Mamie . . . constantly. To make sure she didn't forget something important, like unplugging an iron or shutting off the stove. But she got worse. Soon she was more than he could handle since he was old himself. They had to move into a nursing home. And I remember visiting them at dinnertime. Great-Grandpa Frank sat across the table from Mamie, with his plate pushed to the side, gently lifting a spoonful at a time from her plate and feeding it to her. And he'd smile at her and wink. He'd take a napkin and wipe her chin. He cared for every part of her life, from zippers she couldn't reach and shoes she couldn't tie, to baths she couldn't take alone. He helped her with toilet duties. And all those years, we never heard him complain a single time. He could have easily said, "Hey, I'm an old man. I've had a hard life. And now I can't even blink with Mamie around, because if I do, she might wander off or hurt herself." But he never complained.

Then there was the day my brother and I visited. Great-Grandpa Frank had his overstuffed chair and he sat in it. We stood in front of him, a lot taller now. And he went through the same stories about the fish and the tree houses. But this time the rocking chair next to him was empty—Mamie wasn't there. He still glanced over out of habit. But she was back in their room, confined to her bed, catatonic.

My great-grandfather stopped his stories and looked up at us with a tear slowly running down his cheek, "You know, boys, Mamie doesn't know who I am anymore." And that was the only complaint we ever heard from him about his bride. All the ways she needed his constant attention didn't bother him. What bothered him was when all those times were over. They were married for seventy years. Seventy anniversaries with the same person. I'm positive that after all those decades, she was not the same girl that he married. She didn't look the same. They couldn't do the things they used to do. They were no longer young and strong. She couldn't even remember who he was. But there was no doubt that my great-grandfather was still crazy in love with her. Because love is not what you feel; it's what you do.

LAUGH LESSON

A great way to prepare for eternity is to respect and love the husband or wife of your youth each day that God allows you to spend together. That's one reason why it's better to aim at happily ever laughter than to aim at happily ever after. And don't let your failures along the way prevent you from staying the course. When you mess up—and you will—find some laughter in the situation and keep going.

Adapted from John's DVD presentation *Wedlocked.* You can find out more about John and inside information about his wife and kids at ***www.John Branyan.com***.

29

Why Can't She Just Lie to Me?

Charles Marshall

When couples get married, few realize they have signed up for a lifelong, on-going, daily seminar in interpersonal communication. Not only are bad communication habits exposed, but good ones are also sometimes employed painfully. Decades into his nuptials, Charles Marshall continues to discover the frontiers of communication.

The other day I asked my wife whether she thought I had put on some weight. She answered, "Yeah, maybe a little." Then she laughed, jiggled one of my love handles, and walked out of the room, calling out, "But I still love you!"

Like that helps.

I was bothered on so many levels that I could only babble incoherently as I readjusted my pants and patted down my handles. But the thing that surprised me even more than her remark and flab jostling was that she hadn't been slightly tempted to lie in order to spare my feelings.